HIGHER MODERN STUDIES

Political Issues in the UK

Frank Cooney & Paul Creaney

D0524941

HODDER
GIBSON
AN HACHETTE UK COMPANY

The Publishers would like to thank the following for permission to reproduce copyright material:

Photo credits
Running head images pp. 1, 38, 78 (left) © Douglas McGilviray/istockphoto.com, (right) © TriggerPhoto/istockphoto.com; p.1 © Andrew Milligan/PA Wire/Press Association Images; p.3 http://www.camdennewjournal.com; p.19 ©Jeremy Selwyn / Evening Standard /Rex Features; p.22 (left) ©Photodisc/Getty Images, (right) © Gordon Saunders – Fotolia; p.25 ©David Hartley/Rex Features; p.26 (left) © Nils Jorgensen/Rex Features, (right) © Jeff J Mitchell/Getty Images; p.30 © PA Archive/Press Association Images; p.33 ©Ken McKay/ITV/Rex Features; p.35 (both) © News Group Newspapers Ltd/News International; p.38 ©Tim Rooke/Rex Features; p.39 ©Rex Features; p.42 © PA Archive/Press Association Images; p.43 © Flying Colours/Getty Images; p.44 © Priscilla Coleman/ Getty Images; p.46 Courtesy of Shabana Mahmood MP; p.49 © PA Archive/Press Association Images; p.54 ©Ken McKay/Rex Features; p.55 © Nils Jorgensen/Rex Features; p.56 (left) ©Taxi/FPG/Getty Images, (right) ©Paul Lovelace/Rex Features; p.57 © AFP/Sean Dempsey/Getty Images; p.59 © David Bebber – WPA Pool/Getty Images; p.61 ©Julian Makey/Rex Features; p.62 © Edmund Sumner / View Pictures/Rex Features; p.64 ©Maggie Hardie/Rex Features; p.65 © Hannah Griffiths/Friends of the Earth International; p.66 ©Susannah Hubert/Rex Features; p.67 (top) © photocreo / Fotolia.com, (bottom) © Alexander – Fotolia; p.69 (top) © Derek Blair/ AFP/Getty Images, (bottom) ©Ray Tang/Rex Features; p.70 © Rex Features; p.71 © Rex Features; p.75 ©Rex Features; p.78 © Steve Lindridge / Alamy; p.80 jack_spellingbacon/CC licence Attibution 2.0 Generic/http://commons.wikimedia.org/wiki/File:Dounreay,_ Caithness,_Scotland-30Aug2008.jpg; p.81 Copyright 2011 Scottish Parliamentary Corporate Body/Andrew Cowan/Scottish Parliament; p.85 Copyright 2011 Scottish Parliamentary Corporate Body/Andrew Cowan/Scottish Parliament; p.86 © Dave Donaldson / Alamy; p.89 © PA Wire/Press Association Images; p.92 Copyright © 2011 Scottish Parliamentary Corporate Body/ Andrew Cowan/ Scottish Parliament; p.93 (left to right) ©Nils Jorgensen/Rex Features, ©James Fraser/Rex Features, © Wattie Cheung/Getty Images, Crown copyright – open government licence/http://www.scotland.gov.uk/About/image-gallery/cabinet/cabinetmembers; p.97 ©Steve Back/Rex Features; p.99 ©KeystoneUSA-ZUMA/Rex Features; p.101 © Jeff J Mitchell/Getty Images; p.102 ©Stockbyte/ Photolibrary Group Ltd; p.103 (top) © Alan Wylie / Alamy, (bottom) © Tim Winterburn; p.104 © adisa – Fotolia; p.111© Elizabeth Hayes; p.113 © John Mitchell; p.116 Reproduced with the kind permission of COSLA; p.118 Crown copyright – open government licence/http:// www.scotland.gov.uk/About/image-gallery/cabinet/cabinetmembers; p.123 (left to right) Reproduced with the kind permission of the Scottish Conservatives, Reproduced with the kind permission of the Scottish Liberal Democrats, Reproduced with the kind permission of the Scottish Labour Party, Reproduced with the kind permission of the Scottish National Party, Reproduced with the kind permission of the Scottish Greens.

Acknowledgements
Page 96 Crown copyright material is reproduced under Class Licence Number C02P0000060 with the permission of the Controller of HMSO.

Every effort has been made to trace all copyright holders, but if any have been inadvertently overlooked the Publishers will be pleased to make the necessary arrangements at the first opportunity.

Although every effort has been made to ensure that website addresses are correct at time of going to press, Hodder Gibson cannot be held responsible for the content of any website mentioned in this book. It is sometimes possible to find a relocated web page by typing in the address of the home page for a website in the URL window of your browser.

Hachette Livre UK's policy is to use papers that are natural, renewable and recyclable products and made from wood grown in sustainable forests. The logging and manufacturing processes are expected to conform to the environmental regulations of the country of origin.

Orders: please contact Bookpoint Ltd, 130 Milton Park, Abingdon, Oxon OX14 4SB. Telephone: (44) 01235 827720. Fax: (44) 01235 400454. Lines are open 9.00–5.00, Monday to Saturday, with a 24-hour message answering service. Visit our website at www.hoddereducation.co.uk. Hodder Gibson can be contacted direct on: Tel: 0141 848 1609; Fax: 0141 889 6315; email: hoddergibson@hodder.co.uk

© Frank Cooney and Paul Creaney 2011
First published in 2011 by
Hodder Gibson, an imprint of Hodder Education,
An Hachette UK Company
2a Christie Street
Paisley PA1 1NB

Impression number   5 4 3 2 1
Year   2014 2013 2012 2011

Cover photo (top) © Eain Scott/iStockphoto, (bottom) © Purepix/Alamy
Illustrations by Jeff Edwards
Typeset in Minion Pro 12pt by Fakenham Prepress Solutions, Fakenham, Norfolk NR21 8NN
Printed in Italy

A catalogue record for this title is available from the British Library

ISBN: 978 1444 124361

Contents

Electoral systems, voting and political attitudes

Elections

Purpose of elections

In a democracy, citizens can participate freely through voting to elect their representatives. It is true that electoral turnout has declined in recent years. The 2006 Power Inquiry initiated by the Joseph Rowntree Trust into the state of political participation in the UK concluded that the public's disillusionment with the main political parties and democratic institutions was undermining our democratic systems. Unfortunately, the 2009 MPs' expenses scandal further eroded public confidence.

Elections provide legitimacy to the winning party and to the political system as a whole. By voting, we give consent even if our candidates lose. We can influence the policies of the different parties, and the government of the day will face accountability at the next election.

The failure of the first-past-the-post (FPTP) electoral system to produce a clear winner in the May 2010 general election once again opened the debate over its relevance in the UK in the twenty-first century. As part of the agreement between the Conservatives and Liberal Democrats, a referendum was held on whether we should adopt the alternative vote (AV) system (see pages 4–5). Under the agreement, the Conservatives were free to campaign against change. Many critics would have preferred the choice to be between FPTP and a proportional representation (PR) system, rather than AV

(a modified version of FPTP). The decision to hold the referendum on the same day as the May 2011 Holyrood elections was criticised in Scotland (see page 102).

Figure 1.1 Voters taking part in the 2011 Holyrood elections ↑

In the past, the UK had only one electoral system – FPTP – and this was used to elect MPs to the House of Commons, councillors to local councils across the UK and representatives to the European Parliament.

However, this is no longer the case. As Table 1.1 indicates, a variety of PR systems now operate within the UK for various elections. In Scotland we elect local councillors using the single transferable vote (STV), a form of PR; we elect our representatives to the European Parliament using the regional list, also a form of PR; we elect Members of the Scottish Parliament (MSPs) using the additional member system (AMS), a mixture of FPTP and PR; and finally

Table 1.1 Electoral systems in use in the UK in 2011

System	Election of	Constituency type (single- or multi-member)
First past the post	House of Commons Local government Councils in England and Wales	Single
Additional member system	Scottish Parliament Welsh Assembly London Assembly	Single and multi
Regional list	European Parliament (not Northern Ireland)	Multi
Single transferable vote	Scottish local government councils Northern Ireland Assembly European Parliament (Northern Ireland only)	Multi

we elect our Members of Parliament (MPs) to the House of Commons using FPTP.

So it is no surprise that there is great debate about what system is best for the UK.

What should an election deliver?

- Should it be an FPTP system that usually helps to deliver a clear winner and strong government, and maintains an effective link between MPs and geographical constituencies?
- Or should it be a PR system that helps to ensure greater proportionality and fairness between votes cast and seats achieved?

First past the post

FPTP is a simple plurality system and is the most important electoral system in the UK because it is used for Westminster general elections. The UK is divided into 650 single-member constituencies, also known as 'seats', and each one elects an MP. The candidate with the most votes becomes the MP.

Table 1.2 illustrates why FPTP is referred to as the 'winner-takes-all' system. In 1992 Sir Russell Johnston won the Inverness East, Nairn and Lochaber seat for the Liberal Democrats with the highest number of votes, which turned out to be only 26 per cent of all the votes cast. As the table shows, 74 per cent of the electorate did not vote for the winning candidate.

Table 1.2 Inverness East, Nairn and Lochaber, 1992

	Share of the vote (%)
Liberal Democrats	26.0
Labour	25.1
Conservative	22.6
SNP	24.7

There are no prizes for coming second in this system. For example, the closest result in the 2010 general election was in the marginal constituency of Hampstead and Kilburn. The winning candidate, Labour's Glenda Jackson, retained the seat with 17,332 votes (32.8 per cent); the Conservative candidate received 17,290 votes (32.7 per cent). In this constituency, the

Figure 1.2 **The declaration in Hampstead and Kilburn in 2010** ↑

difference between success and failure was only 42 votes. This is even more remarkable when you consider that on average each constituency has about 70,000 voters.

Differences in the size of constituencies can reflect geographic factors. The Isle of Wight has the most electors and the Western Isles the fewest. Historically Scotland has been over-represented,

and the number of Scottish constituencies was reduced from 72 to 59 in 2005.

The bill to hold the May 2011 referendum on electoral reform, which was part of the coalition deal between the Conservatives and Liberal Democrats, also included plans to redraw constituency boundaries to create as far as possible numerically equal constituencies of around 75,000 voters. (The two main exceptions are the Scottish seats of Orkney and Shetland, and the Western Isles.) This proposal will reduce the number of constituencies from 650 seats to 600 and will favour the Conservative Party. Independent experts have calculated that with 50 fewer MPs Labour would lose around 27, the Conservatives around 12, the Liberal Democrats around 5 and other parties the remaining 6.

Features of FPTP

Maintains a two-party system

FPTP ensures that the proportion of seats won by Conservative and Labour is far greater than

Table 1.3 **The British two-party system, selected years**

	Share of the vote (%)			Share of the seats (%)			Liberal / Liberal Democrats		Overall majority
	Con	Lab	Con + Lab	Con	Lab	Con + Lab	Votes (%)	Seats (%)	
1951	48.0	**48.8**	96.8	51.4	47.2	98.6	2.5	1.0	17
1974	**37.9**	37.1	75.0	46.6	47.4	94.0	19.3	2.2	–
1974	35.8	39.2	75.0	43.5	50.2	93.7	18.3	2.0	3
1983	**42.4**	27.6	70.0	61.0	32.2	93.2	25.4	3.6	144
1992	**41.9**	34.4	76.3	51.6	41.6	93.2	17.9	3.1	21
1997	30.7	**43.2**	73.9	25.0	63.6	88.6	16.8	7.0	179
2001	31.7	**40.7**	72.4	25.1	62.6	87.7	18.8	7.9	167
2005	32.4	**35.2**	67.6	30.7	54.9	85.6	22.9	9.6	64
2010	36.1	29.0	65.1	47.2	38.7	85.9	23.0	8.9	–

The figures in bold denote the share of the vote of the party which won the most seats in the House of Commons. In 1951 and 1974 the party with the most votes did not win the most seats the proportion of votes they receive. In the 2010 general election the combined Conservative/Labour vote was 65.1 per cent yet they received 85.9 per cent of the seats (see Table 1.3). Some political commentators argue that FPTP acts as a life-support machine for the two-party system and distorts the will of the electorate.

Comfortable government

FPTP usually exaggerates the performance of the most popular party and provides it with a comfortable majority in parliament.

The Conservatives under Margaret Thatcher enjoyed landslide victories in 1983 and 1987, as did Labour under Tony Blair in 1997 and 2001.

Unfair to smaller parties

FPTP discriminates against third parties and smaller parties whose support is spread across the UK but is not concentrated in particular regions. The Liberal Democrats have consistently suffered: there are no rewards for coming second in, for example, 300 constituencies. In the 2010 general election, the Liberal Democrats won 23 per cent of the vote but received only 57 seats; in contrast, Labour won 29 per cent of the vote and received 307 seats.

The Green Party did manage to win their first ever seat in the 2010 general election. The Liberal Democrats and the smaller parties increased their number of seats to 85, making up 13 per cent of the total seats, but this was not a fair return for 25 per cent of the votes.

Limited choice

Many constituencies are **safe seats**, in which one party has a massive majority over its rivals and is unlikely to lose. All of Glasgow's Westminster constituencies are held by Labour, and the Conservatives do very badly. Why should a Conservative supporter bother to vote when his or her vote will be of no consequence? Voters whose favoured party has little support might engage in **tactical voting**. Instead of voting

for their party, electors cast their votes for the candidate best placed to prevent a party they dislike from winning the seat.

Favours the Labour Party

Labour's vote is distributed more efficiently than that of other parties, especially in Scotland (see Table 1.4). In 2005, Labour won a majority of 66 seats with 35 per cent of the votes, yet in the 2010 general election the Conservatives were 19 seats short of a parliamentary majority with 36 per cent of the votes.

Traditionally the Liberal Democrats fare better in Scotland than in the rest of the UK because part of their support is concentrated in rural areas such as the Highlands. In 2010 the SNP vote was 491,386 compared to the Liberal Democrats' 465,471 – yet the Liberal Democrats won eleven seats and the SNP only six. In Scotland the Conservatives won 17 per cent of the vote but only one of the 59 seats, with Labour taking about 70 per cent of Scottish seats on 42 per cent of the vote.

Table 1.4 **Average number of votes needed to win a constituency at the 2010 general election**

Party	Number of votes	
	UK	**Scotland**
Conservative	35,000	412,850
Labour	33,500	25,250
Liberal Democrats	120,000	42,315
SNP	–	81,897

Clearly, in Scotland FPTP favours Labour and is most unfair to the Conservatives.

Alternative vote

This is the electoral system proposed by the Liberal Democrats to replace FPTP. This seems a strange choice for the Liberal Democrats because AV is, in effect, only a modified form of

Table 1.5 **The number of seats won by each party in the 2010 general election under different voting systems**

Party	First past the post	Alternative vote	Single transferable vote
Conservative	307	281	246
Labour	258	262	207
Liberal Democrats	57	79	162
Others	28	28	38

FPTP. Research by the Electoral Reform Society indicates that the Liberal Democrats would have won an additional 22 seats if AV had been used in the 2010 general election, and 105 more under STV (see Table 1.5).

AV is used to elect Australia's lower house, the House of Representatives, and in the UK it is used to elect the leader of the Labour Party and Liberal Democrats.

In AV the winning candidate has to achieve an overall majority of the votes cast. Voters write '1' beside the name of their first-choice candidate, '2' next to their second choice and so on. Voters may decide to vote only for their first choice. If no candidate has secured an absolute majority of first preferences, the lowest-placed candidate drops out and the second preferences of his or her votes are transferred to the remaining candidates. If this does not produce a candidate with more than 50 per cent of the votes, the procedure will be repeated until it does.

Table 1.5 clearly indicates why the Conservatives, even though they are in coalition with the Liberal Democrats, campaigned against AV: it would favour both the Labour Party and the Liberal Democrats, thus making it more difficult for the Conservatives to achieve an overall majority.

Alternative Vote referendum May 2011

The country voted 'No' to changing the electoral system and chose to continue to support a FPTP system that they understood. The Liberal Democrats and the 'Yes' campaign failed to match the impact of the 'No' campaign supported by the Conservative Party and some Labour politicians, such as John Reid. No region had a majority of 'Yes' votes; only in Northern Ireland did the 'Yes' vote muster a respectable figure (see Table 1.6). Of the 440 UK voting areas only 10, including Glasgow Kelvin and Edinburgh Central, voted 'Yes'.

The turnout at the referendum was also low, reflecting the 'Yes' campaign's failure to capture the interest of the public. It was clear that much of the public did not understand the Alternative Vote System. Northern Ireland had the highest turnout at 56 per cent, followed by Scotland at 51 per cent. London had the lowest turnout at only 35 per cent. The highest turnout for a voting area

Advantages of AV

- It would not require any boundary changes and the constituencies would still return one MP.

- All MPs would have gained the majority of the votes and they would have broader support.

Disadvantages of AV

- The candidate who secures the most first-preference votes may not be elected when second or third preferences have been distributed.

- It retains all the weaknesses of FPTP and is still unfair to third and minority parties.

was Eastwood, in East Renfrewshire, at 63 per cent, and the lowest was Newham in London.

The Liberal Democrats were also unhappy at the tactics of the 'No' campaign and the Conservative leaders. At the beginning of the campaign David Cameron indicated he would not fight Mr Clegg head to head over the referendum. However, early 2011 opinion polls gave the 'Yes' vote a clear lead and to placate the right-wingers in his party Mr Cameron threw his weight behind the 'No' campaign.

The Prime Minister did not disown the blatant lies proclaimed by the 'No' campaign – that new ballot boxes would be needed, that the cost of AV would be astronomical and that a party that came last, such as the British National Party (BNP), could end up having the winning candidate. However, Labour did not blame the Conservatives for the failed referendum. Labour's Ben Bradshaw tweeted: 'Done countless AV meetings in recent months. Two words sum up the reason for the scale of defeats: Nick Clegg. Toxic. Specially with Labour voters.'

Activities

1 Describe the different electoral systems used in the UK.

2 Why is the UK electoral system referred to as first past the post?

3 Refer to Table 1.3. Examine the statements below and indicate to what extent you agree, or disagree, with each:
   (a) There has been a significant decline in support for the two major parties.
   (b) All elections since 1951 have produced a clear winner.
   (c) The Liberal Democrats have been unfairly treated by FPTP.

4 Outline the main features of FPTP.

5 Why did the Conservative Party oppose the introduction of AV? Refer to Table 1.5 in your answer.

6 Outline the advantages and disadvantages of AV.

7 Examine the results of the 2011 referendum.

Table 1.6 **AV referendum results by UK voting areas, May 2011**

Voting area	Yes (%)	No (%)	Turnout (%)
Scotland	36.36	63.64	50.74
Northern Ireland	43.68	56.32	55.79
North East	28.05	71.95	38.73
North West	30.22	69.78	39.10
Yorkshire and the Humber	31.29	68.71	39.92
Wales	34.55	65.45	41.74
West Midlands	28.52	71.48	39.82
East Midlands	28.74	71.26	42.77
South West	31.54	68.46	44.61
South East	29.68	70.32	44.31
London	39.53	60.47	35.37
Eastern	29.00	71.00	43.15

Arguments for FPTP

1 It exaggerates the performance of the most popular party, producing a winners' dividend and even a landslide victory. In 1997, Labour won 43 per cent of the vote and gained 419 seats in the House of Commons, giving them a massive majority.

2 Strong single-party government allows the prime minister and cabinet to pursue the policies they stated clearly in their election manifesto without having to compromise with smaller parties in the coalitions associated with PR.

3 FPTP prevents extremist parties from obtaining representation. The British National Party (BNP) achieved over half a million votes in the 2010 general election but gained no seats. Under a PR system, the BNP won two seats in the 2009 European elections.

4 When an MP retires or dies, a by-election is held to elect a new MP. This enables the public to show their disapproval of a government or party in government that has become unpopular. In March 2011, the Liberal Democrats slumped to sixth in the Barnsley Central by-election. Their vote fell from 17 per cent to a humiliating 4 per cent.

5 It is easy to understand and implement. Electors only vote once and the results are announced very quickly. In contrast, there were 140,000 spoilt ballot papers in the 2007 Scottish Parliament elections.

Arguments against FPTP

1 The two-party system is past its sell-by date because it no longer reflects voting patterns. In the 1950s, over 90 per cent of the electorate voted for either of the two major parties; in the 2010 general election, only 65 per cent voted for either the Conservatives or Labour. It is unfair to third and minority parties: in 1983, the third party (Liberal–SDP Alliance) gained 25 per cent of the votes and less than 4 per cent of seats.

2 FPTP does not always produce a victory for the party with the most votes or deliver a fair or decisive result. In the February 1974 election, the Conservatives gained more votes than Labour yet had fewer seats (see Table 1.3). In the 2005 election, Labour formed a government with only 35.2 per cent of the votes cast. *The Independent* newspaper described it as 'the most unfair election result of all time' because this was the lowest ever share of the vote for a winning party. And in 2010, it failed to deliver a decisive outcome.

3 Strong government does not always create a good or fair government. When FPTP was used in the elections in Northern Ireland, the leader of the Ulster Unionists made the infamous statement 'a Protestant government for a Protestant people'. This abuse of power denied Northern Irish Catholics their civil and political rights. Today in Northern Ireland, under a PR system (STV), there is a power-sharing government between the Democratic Unionist Party and Sinn Fein.

4 The winning MP may not have a majority of the votes cast; indeed, they may receive less than 30 per cent of the vote. In 1992, the Liberal Democrat candidate in Inverness East, Nairn and Lochaber won with 26 per cent of the vote (see Table 1.2).

5 Some people argue that FPTP leads to voter apathy because it creates electoral deserts. The Conservatives won 17 per cent of the Scottish votes in 2010 but only one seat.

Arguments for PR

1 PR is 'fair' because it produces a close correlation between share of the vote and share of seats.

2 PR gives minor parties more parliamentary representation and encourages voters to vote for them without feeling that their votes will be wasted. In the 2003 elections for the Scottish Parliament, AMS enabled the Scottish Socialist Party (SSP), the Green Party, the Scottish Senior Citizens Unity Party and the independents to be represented.

3 Coalition government increases the percentage of the electorate supporting the government parties. In the 2010 general election, the coalition Conservative–Liberal Democrat government won a combined 59 per cent of votes. (Although the Scottish electorate might see it differently!)

4 Coalitions encourage consensus, which is the result of compromise. In other words, more voters get some of what they want and less of what they do not want. The Liberal Democrats and Labour formed a coalition government in Scotland in 1999–2007, providing stable and effective government.

5 Some people argue that PR will reduce the number of 'wasted votes' and so encourage greater turnout.

Arguments against PR

1 PR can create a government in which a minority party can implement its policies. The Liberal Democrats finished fourth in the 2003 Scottish election, yet formed a government with Labour. When they formed a coalition with the Conservatives in May 2010, the Liberal Democrats dropped their manifesto pledges such as no increase in student fees.

2 PR can lead to an unstable and weak government. The minority SNP government of 2007–11 found it difficult to implement some of its policies. For example, it failed to implement its policy of minimum pricing of alcohol in November 2010.

3 PR does not always create a more representative Scottish Parliament. In the 2007 Scottish elections, the number of MSPs outwith the four major parties decreased from 17 to 3.

4 Some people argue that AMS creates conflict between the constituency MSP and the seven list MSPs. There is clear rivalry between the two classes of MSPs. (See page 87.)

5 The regional list system makes parties more powerful than voters. Being placed first or second on your party's list will mean you have a very good chance of being elected to the Scottish Parliament (assuming you represent one of the major parties). Margo MacDonald, a leading SNP figure, decided to stand as an independent on the Lothian regional list after she had been given a low place on the SNP's party list.

The additional member system

This mixed electoral system has been used to elect the Scottish Parliament and Welsh Assembly since 1999, and also in the London Assembly. In Scotland the voters cast two votes. The first vote is to elect the 73 winning candidates in the local constituency elections using FPTP.

They also have a second vote in a multi-member constituency, choosing between parties. Scotland is divided into eight regional lists, each electing seven regional list MSPs (see Figure 1.3). The d'Hondt formula is used to ensure that the number of seats for parties in the Scottish Parliament is roughly proportional to the number of votes they won. A party that has a clear lead in the constituency election will do less well in the regional list elections. In 2007 Labour won 37 constituency seats but only 9 regional list seats.

The outcome is that a single party hardly ever wins a majority of seats. AMS ensured the creation of Labour and Liberal Democrat coalition governments after the 1999 and 2003 elections and of a minority SNP government after the 2007 election. The impact of AMS on the government of Scotland is discussed further in Chapter 3. The 2011 Scottish Parliament results are highlighted on pages 11–13.

Impact of the new voting system

AMS, incorporating a strong element of PR, was introduced to reduce the alleged deficiencies of FPTP. What have been the principal consequences for Scottish politics of its operation since 1999?

A fairer result

There is no doubt that AMS increases proportionality by reducing the gap between share of votes and share of seats (see Table 1.6). In sharp contrast, in 2010 the FPTP system awarded Labour almost 70 per cent of Scottish seats in the House of Commons with only 42 per cent of the Scottish vote.

Coalition government or minority-party government

In 1999 and 2003, Labour formed a coalition government with the Liberal Democrats.

In the 2007 election, the SNP overtook Labour as the strongest party in the Scottish Parliament, but only by a single seat. The SNP could not find a coalition partner with enough seats to provide a parliamentary majority because of its stated intention to hold a referendum on independence. The SNP formed a minority government and had to depend on other parties supporting their policies for the respective bills to be passed in parliament.

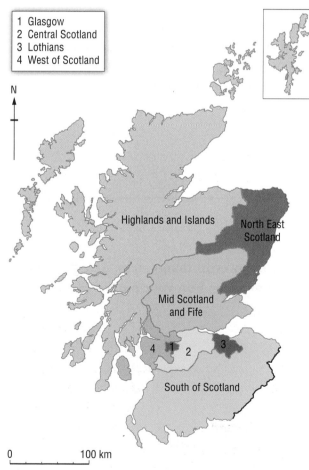

1 Glasgow
2 Central Scotland
3 Lothians
4 West of Scotland

N

Highlands and Islands

North East Scotland

Mid Scotland and Fife

4 1 2 3

South of Scotland

0   100 km

Figure 1.3 The eight multi-member constituencies in Scotland ↑

Small parties encouraged and sometimes rewarded

In 2003, the Greens and the SSP won 13 out of 56 seats in the second ballot. The presence of Green and SSP MSPs in the Scottish Parliament would not have been achieved under FPTP. This feature has been erratic in so far as the significant gains of both the Greens and the SSP in 2003 were almost eliminated in 2007, when they lost votes and seats as the SNP surged into first place. Thanks to AMS, the Greens hung on with two list seats – one each in Glasgow and the Lothians.

Greater voter choice

There has been a large increase in the number of parties and individual candidates competing for seats in the second ballot. No fewer than 23 parties and independents contested the second ballot in both Glasgow and the Lothians in 2007.

The second ballot and an increase in the number of parties have given voters the opportunity to vote for more than one party.

However, the 2007 results emphasise that smaller parties are not guaranteed representation if the battle between the major parties intensifies, meaning that their share of the second-ballot regional vote falls below 5–6 per cent.

Parties rewarded for votes achieved

AMS has maintained the four-party character of Scottish politics by coming to the rescue of the Conservatives. The Conservatives won only one seat in the 2010 general election; in contrast, they have 15 MSPs in the new Scottish Parliament of 2011.

Gender representation in the Scottish Parliament

One of the most striking features of the first election to the Scottish Parliament in 1999 was that 48 of the 129 MSPs were women – 37 per cent of the total membership. This was double the proportion of women in the House of Commons and close to the 40 per cent achieved in Sweden.

In 2007 there were only 43 female MSPs. Labour had the highest proportion of

Table 1.7 **Scottish Parliament election results, 2003**

Party	Constituency MSPs	Regional list MSPs	Total MSPs	Votes (%)	Seats (%)
Labour	46	4	50	31.9	38.8
SNP	9	18	27	22.3	20.9
Liberal Democrats	13	4	17	13.6	13.2
Conservative	3	15	18	16.0	14.0
Green	0	7	7	6.9	5.4
SSP	0	6	6	6.4	4.7
Save Stobhill Hospital Party	1	0	1	0.6	0.8
Scottish Senior Citizens Unity Party	0	1	1	0.8	0.8
Independents	1	1	2	1.5	1.6
Total	**73**	**56**	**129**	**100**	**100**

Turnout: 49.4%

female MSPs: exactly 50 per cent of Labour representation at Holyrood. More than half of the Labour MSPs elected in the first ballot were women. Labour and the SNP were more successful than other parties at getting women elected in the first ballot.

Electorate confusion

The May 2007 Scottish Parliament and local council elections created confusion among the electorate. A change to the ballot papers for the parliamentary elections and a switch from FPTP to STV for local council elections seemed to confuse some voters. In the 2003 elections there had been 45,700 rejected ballot papers; in the 2007 elections, a staggering 140,000 were rejected.

Scottish Parliament Election May 2011

Alex Salmond's landslide victory took everyone by surprise. In January 2010 early opinion polls gave Labour a clear 16 points lead. This was confirmed in the 2010 General Election when Scottish Labour easily dismissed the SNP challenge and, in fact, Scotland was the only part of the UK where Labour's vote increased (see page 27).

When the Scottish Parliament elections came around in May 2011, the SNP gained 22 seats and achieved what was regarded as impossible under the proportional voting system – an overall majority of seats: 69 out of 129. In the north east, the SNP won all 10 constituency seats, and still obtained another on the regional list (see Table 1.14). The results were all the more remarkable given that in the 1999 election the then-dominant Labour Party only achieved 56 seats.

A Labour aide, speaking after the results were announced, described the situation as 'ground zero', especially for several high profile MSPs. Labour's decision not to use the regional list as a saftey net for the party heayweights left it

without its most experienced and talented MSPs: Andy Kerr, Tom McCabe and David Whitton, to name but three, all lost their constituency seats.

Labour's constituency vote had declined by only 0.5 per cent and its regional vote by 3 per cent in an election where the turnout was 50 per cent – 1.3 per cent less than than in 2007. So why did the party suffer such heavy losses? It is clear that the collapse of the Liberal Democrat vote benefitted the SNP rather than Labour. Scottish voters punished the Liberal Democrats for their coalition with the Conservatives in Westminster and the party was reduced from 16 MSPs to 5, with no mainland constituency MSPs. (Shetland and Orkney returned the two Liberal Democrat constituency MSPs, including the then-leader Tavish Scott.) Overall the party's vote slumped below half its 2007 level with Liberal Democrat disaffected voters switching to the SNP.

It was also a disappointing result for the Conservatives and a slight disappointment for the Greens. Conservative support fell to its lowest level of support in Scotland and lost two of its MSPs. Annabel Goldie, Conservative leader since 2005, resigned, as did Labour's Ian Gray and Tavish Scott of the Liberal Democrats. The number of Green MSPs did not increase after the election but they were able to retain their two MSPs .

Why did Labour suffer such a massive defeat?

1 The original strategy to ignore the SNP and instead campaign against the UK coalition and the return to Thatcherism was a disaster. The tactics which worked in the 2010 General Election failed to impress the electorate this time around.

2 The SNP campaign confirmed Alex Salmond's popularity and leadership qualities. In a YouGov poll in April 2011, 52 per cent of those asked said

Mr Salmond would make the best First Minster. Only 27 per cent chose Mr Gray, the Labour leader, regarded as the invisable, dull politician.

3 The collapse of the Liberal Democrat vote benefitted the SNP rather than Labour, dramatically changing the Scottish political map (see Figures 1.4 and 1.5). The Liberal Democrats lost 11 of their 16 MSPs and retained only their constituency MSPs in Orkney and Shetland. Labour's constituency votes remained solid with only a 0.5 per cent reduction, yet they lost 22 of their constituency MSPs.

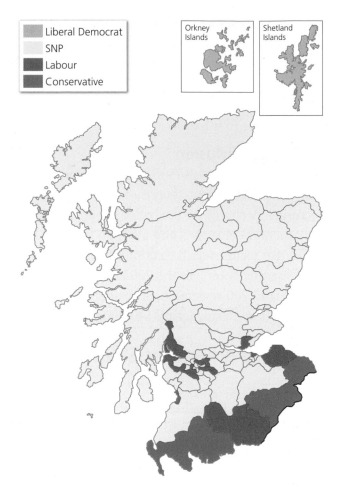

Figure 1.5 Scottish Parliament election results 2011 ↑

National/regional party list

This PR system was introduced for elections to the European Parliament in England, Scotland and Wales in 1999 (but not in Northern Ireland). Here the electorate do not vote for individual party candidates but for a party. Political parties draw up a list of candidates in the order in which they will be elected. Representatives are elected from 11 large multi-member regions, each electing between 3 and 10 MEPs. In the 2009 European election, Scotland elected 6 MEPs (see Tables 1.14 and 1.15).

The 2009 European Parliament election saw the UK Independence Party (UKIP) receiving more votes than Labour across the UK, a severe embarrassment for the Labour Government of Gordon Brown. One negative outcome of the PR

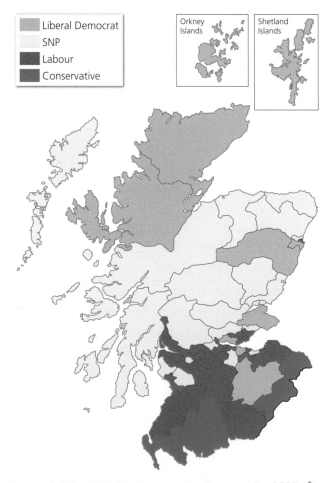

Figure 1.4 Scottish Parliament election results 2007 ↑

Table 1.8 Scottish Parliament election results, 2007

Party	Constituency MSPs	Share of vote (%)	Regional list MSPs	Share of vote (%)	Total MSPs
SNP	21	32.9	26	31.0	47
Labour	37	32.2	9	29.2	46
Conservative	4	16.6	13	13.9	17
Liberal Democrats	11	16.2	5	11.3	16
Green	0	0.15	2	4.0	2
Total	**73**		**56**		**129**

Turnout: 51.7%

Table 1.9 Summary of total MSPs by party from 1999 to 2011

Party	1999	2003	2007	2011
SNP	35	27	47	69
Labour	56	50	46	37
Conservative	18	18	17	15
Liberal Democrats	17	17	16	5
Green	1	7	2	2
SSP	1	6	0	0
Others	1	4	1	1

Table 1.10 European election results, 2009: UK

Party	Votes		MEPs	
	Total	%	Total	+/-
Conservative	4,198,394	27.7 (+1.0)	25	+1
UKIP	2,498,226	16.5 (+0.3)	13	+1
Labour	2,381,760	15.7 (−6.9)	13	−5
Liberal Democrats	2,080,613	13.7 (−1.2)	11	+1
Green	1,303,745	8.6 (+2.4)	2	0
BNP	943,598	6.2 (+1.3)	2	+2
SNP	321,007	2.1 (+0.7)	2	0

Seats: 72   Turnout: 15,625,823 (34.5%)   Electorate: 45,315,669

Table 1.11 Scottish Parliament election results May 2011

Party	SNP	+/–	Lab	+/–	Cons	+/–	Lib Dem	+/–	Others	+/–
Total	69	+22	37	–9	15	–2	5	–11	3	–

Table 1.12 Scottish Parliament election May 2011 constituency results

Party	Seats	+/–	Votes	%	+/– %
SNP	53	+32	902,915	45.4	+12.5
Labour	15	–20	630,461	31.7	–0.5
Conservative	3	–3	276,652	13.9	–2.7
Liberal Democrats	2	–9	157,714	7.9	–8.2
Others	0	0	21,480	1.1	–1.1

Table 1.13 Scottish Parliament election May 2011 regional list results

Party	Seats	+/–	Votes	%	+/– %
SNP	16	–9	876,421	44	+13
Labour	22	+13	523,559	26.3	–2.9
Conservative	12	–2	245,967	12.4	–1.6
Liberal Democrats	3	–3	103,472	5.2	–6.1
Others	3	+1	241,632	12.1	–2.5

Table 1.14 Scottish Parliament election May 2011 parliamentary region results

Region	SNP	Labour	Conservative	Liberal Democrats	Green	Others
Highlands and Islands	9	2	2	2		
North East Scotland	11	3	2	1		
Mid Scotland and Fife	9	4	2	1		
Central	9	6	1			
Lothians	8	4	2		1	1
Glasgow	7	7	1		1	
West of Scotland	8	7	2			
South Scotland	8	4	3	1		
Total	69	37	15	5	2	1

Table 1.15 European election results, 2009: Scotland

Party	Votes		MEPs (total)
	Total	**%**	
SNP	321,007	29.1	2
Labour	229,853	20.8	2
Conservative	185,794	16.8	1
Liberal Democrats	127,038	11.5	1
Green	80,442	7.3	0
UKIP	57,788	5.2	0

nature of this election was the success of the BNP in gaining two seats with only 6.2 per cent of the votes. The Liberal Democrats witnessed a slight decline in their votes, yet increased their representation in the European Parliament to 11.

In Scotland, a different picture emerged. UKIP received only 5 per cent of the votes and no seats. The SNP received the most votes – almost 30 per cent – but still did not increase their number of seats. Labour received the same number of seats as the SNP with 20 per cent of the votes. Again the BNP made no advance in Scotland, receiving 2.5 per cent of the votes and no seats.

Single transferable vote

This PR system was used in the Scottish local government elections for the first time in May 2007. It is also used in Northern Ireland for elections to both the Northern Ireland Assembly and the European Parliament.

The main features of STV are:

1 Representatives are chosen from multi-member constituencies. In a five-member local government constituency (ward), voters rank their preferences among the candidates using the figures 1–5. Often the number of candidates will be in double figures.
2 Electors can vote for as many or as few candidates as they like.
3 A complicated quota system is used to calculate the minimum number of votes required to win one of the seats. The quota is calculated by dividing the number of votes cast by the number of seats available plus one. In a four-member constituency where 150,000 votes were cast, a candidate would require 30,001 votes in order to be elected. Any votes in excess of this quota are redistributed on the basis of second preferences.

Advantages of the regional list

- There is greater proportionality between votes cast and seats gained. In the 2004 European elections, which used FPTP, Labour gained 44 per cent of the vote and received 74 per cent of the seats.

- It rewards smaller parties. In the 2010 European elections, UKIP won 16.5 per cent of the vote and received 13 seats (the same as Labour).

Disadvantages of the regional list

- The link between representatives and constituents is weakened in large multi-member constituencies. Very few people in Scotland could name their MEP.

STV formula

$$\text{Quota of votes} = \frac{\text{Number of votes cast} + 1}{\text{Number of seats} + 1}$$

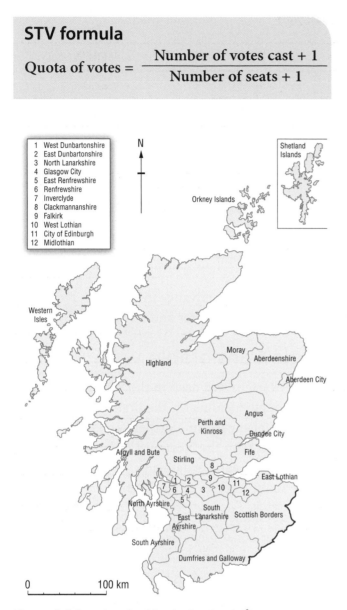

1 West Dunbartonshire
2 East Dunbartonshire
3 North Lanarkshire
4 Glasgow City
5 East Renfrewshire
6 Renfrewshire
7 Inverclyde
8 Clackmannanshire
9 Falkirk
10 West Lothian
11 City of Edinburgh
12 Midlothian

Figure 1.6 Local authorities in Scotland ↑

The 2007 Scottish local government elections

In May 2007, the STV system was used for local government elections in Scotland to elect councillors to multi-member wards consisting of three or four members. These multi-member wards are larger geographical areas and therefore councillors represent wider groups of people. However, the total number of councillors remains unchanged.

The Local Governance (Scotland) Act (2004) facilitated this change from the traditional FPTP system to a form of PR. It resulted in substantial change in both the composition and political control of Scottish local authorities.

The first significant change happened even before the election took place: a large number of councillors did not stand for re-election in 2007. Consequently, there was a significant change to the personnel elected with almost half (48 per cent) being elected for the first time. The Local Governance (Scotland) Act (2004) established remuneration arrangements for councillors and provided for severance payments to be made to those who were not standing for re-election in 2007. There was also a significant decrease in the number of candidates standing for election (see Table 1.16). It is clear that the parties did not wish to divide their potential vote by having too many candidates.

However, the most significant factor in the change from using FPTP to using STV was the results of previous elections. In 2007 Labour either lost control of councils or had to run them as a minority, whereas the old system of FPTP had given them comfortable majorities in councils such as East Lothian, Midlothian, Stirling and Clackmannanshire. Overall, there was a dramatic reduction in Labour council representation and an increase in the number of SNP councillors in almost every council. Only Glasgow and North Lanarkshire remained under Labour majority-administration control, while Orkney, Shetland and the Western Isles continued to be controlled by independent councillors.

Losers

Table 1.17 clearly shows the decline of Labour's dominance at local elections. Labour had the largest fall in representation at local authority level, with 161 fewer councillors being elected in 2007 compared to 2003.

Table 1.16 **Number of candidates in local council elections, 1999–2007**

	1999	**2003**	**2007**
Number of candidates	3,934	4,195	2,607
Number of seats	1,222	1,222	1,222

Table 1.17 **Local council election results, 2007**

Party	**No. of councillors**	**Net gain/loss compared with 2003 elections**
SNP	363	+182
Labour	348	−161
Liberal Democrats	166	−9
Conservative	143	+20
Green	8	+8
SSP	1	−1
Solidarity	1	+1
Independent and others	192	−42
Total	**1,222**	

'Others', which consist mainly of independent councillors, also lost out with 42 fewer councillors.

It seems that the change in the voting system and a perceived resurgence in the influence of party politics have deepened the decline of independent councillors. In Aberdeenshire, Moray, Dumfries and Galloway, and the Scottish Borders the number of independent councillors was cut dramatically in 2007. For example, in Dumfries and Galloway only 2 independent councillors won seats compared to 12 in 2003.

Winners

The main winners were the SNP, who gained 182 councillors. In 2003 the SNP had 25 per cent of votes but only 15 per cent of seats, in contrast to Labour with 33 per cent of votes and 42 per cent of seats. The Conservatives had twenty more councillors than in 2003 and the Greens also gained their first eight councillors.

Control of councils

In 2003 there were 20 local authorities with single-party 'majority' administrations. Labour controlled thirteen local authorities, the SNP one and the independents six, with eleven run by coalitions.

In 2007 things were entirely different. There were only five local authorities with single-party 'majority' administrations. Two were Labour (Glasgow City and North Lanarkshire), three were formed by a group of independents and six were run by single-party minority administrations. The remaining 21 local authorities had multi-party coalitions forming a governing administration.

The impact of PR on the 2007 Scottish local council elections

There was a modest increase in turnout from 49.6 per cent in 2003 to 53.8 per cent in 2007. However, this was still significantly lower than the 58.1 per cent turnout under FPTP in 1999. It should be noted that in 1999 the electorate were also voting to elect a Scottish Parliament for the first time, and this obviously increased local government turnout.

Out of 32 councils 27 were left with no single party being in overall control, while only Glasgow City and North Lanarkshire remained in Labour hands after the use of STV.

Labour's influence declined: it was no longer the majority party in many local authority areas including East Lothian, Midlothian, Clackmannanshire and Stirling councils.

The increase in the number of councillors from small parties and the levelling out of results for parties other than Labour has been attributed to the use of PR.

Labour kept control of Glasgow City Council with 45 councillors; the SNP won 22, the Liberal Democrats and Greens 5 each, and Solidarity and the Conservatives had one councillor each.

In both Aberdeen and Aberdeenshire, the Liberal Democrats remained the biggest single party. There was no single majority party on either council, leaving both councils with no overall control. In Aberdeen the Liberal Democrats had fifteen councillors, the SNP twelve, Labour ten and the Conservatives five, with one independent. In Aberdeenshire the Liberal Democrats had 24 councillors, the SNP 22 and the Conservatives 14, with 8 independents.

No single party had overall control in Midlothian, with nine Labour, six SNP and three Liberal Democrat councillors. Prior to the use of STV, on the old council Labour controlled 14 out of the 18 wards.

In Stirling, where control of the council has always been finely balanced – having twice been decided by the cutting of cards – the use of STV in 2007 resulted in Labour gaining eight wards on the new council to the SNP's seven, the Conservatives' four and the Liberal Democrats' three.

In East Lothian, Labour gained seven councillors, as did the SNP; the Liberal Democrats had six and the Conservatives two, with one independent. Prior to the use of STV, Labour controlled 16 out of the 23 wards.

In Angus the SNP lost overall control after running the council since 1995, dropping from 17 wards to 13 on a council of 29.

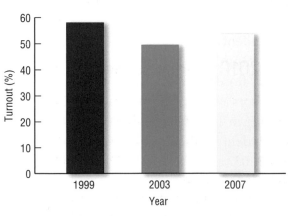

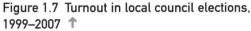

Figure 1.7 Turnout in local council elections, 1999–2007 ↑

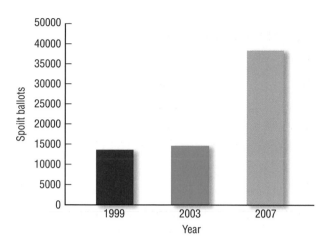

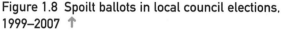

Figure 1.8 Spoilt ballots in local council elections, 1999–2007 ↑

Activities

1 Describe briefly how AMS works in Scotland.

2 AMS ensures a fairer distribution of seats and a greater choice for the electorate. To what extent did the 2003 and 2007 Scottish Parliament elections achieve this outcome?

3 Describe how the national/regional party list system operates and its impact on the political parties in the 2004 and 2009 European elections.

4 Describe briefly how the STV system operates.

5 Outline the impact of STV on the Scottish local council elections of 2007.

The 2010 general election

The Conservatives prevented Labour from winning four general elections in a row but it was to be no landslide victory for the Conservatives and no breakthrough by the Liberal Democrats.

The most significant feature of the 2010 general election was the failure of FPTP to deliver on its main promise – a single-party government. The last time a hung parliament had occurred was in February 1974.

A total of 326 seats is needed for a party to cross the winning line in a 650-seat parliament, thereby forming a majority government. The Conservatives won a total of 307 seats and achieved a 5 per cent swing from Labour; an impressive performance, but not the conclusive victory that they required.

The Conservatives did not attempt to form a minority government. Instead they persuaded the Liberal Democrats to enter a formal coalition with David Cameron (the Conservative leader) as prime minister and Nick Clegg (the Lib Dem leader) as deputy prime minister. The Conservatives also offered to hold a referendum on the introduction of the AV system to replace FPTP.

Figure 1.9 David Cameron and Nick Clegg formed a coalition government ↑

The key statistics of the 2010 general election illustrate the contrasting fortunes of the major parties:

- The Conservatives gained 87 seats from Labour and 12 from the Liberal Democrats.
- Labour's 29 per cent share of the UK vote was only slightly better than the party's post-war low in 1983.
- The drift away from the 'old two-party system'

continued: only two in three of all votes cast were for the two major parties.

- Five million fewer people voted for Labour compared to their 1997 landslide victory.
- The number of ethnic-minority MPs increased from 14 to 27.
- The Conservatives failed once again to make progress in Scotland. They remained the fourth-placed party with only one MP.
- The Green Party gained their first MP, Caroline Lucas. All three sitting independent MPs were defeated.
- Despite Nick Clegg's 'victory' in the televised debates, the Liberal Democrats witnessed only a small rise in their share of the vote and a net loss of five seats.

Activity

1 The 2010 general election was a triumph for the Conservatives and a disaster for all other parties. To what extent do you agree with this statement? To what extent are the Scottish results different from the UK results?

2 To what extent was the 2011 Scottish Parliament election a triumph for the SNP and a disaster for all the other parties?

Essay questions

1 Compare and contrast the advantages of the electoral systems used to elect the UK and Scottish Parliaments.

2 STV gives the electorate better representation and more choice than FPTP. Discuss.

Table 1.18 **Result of the 2010 general election**

Party	Seats	Gain	Loss	Net	Votes	Vote (%)	+/−
Conservative	**307**	100	3	+97	10,726,614	36.1	+3.8
Labour	**258**	3	94	−91	8,609,527	29.0	−6.2
Liberal Democrats	**57**	8	13	−5	6,836,824	23.0	+1.0
Democratic Unionist Party	**8**	0	1	−1	168,216	0.6	−0.3
SNP	**6**	0	0	0	491,386	1.7	+0.1
Sinn Fein	**5**	0	0	0	171,942	0.6	−0.1
Plaid Cymru	**3**	1	0	+1	165,394	0.6	−0.1
Social Democratic and Labour Party	**3**	0	0	0	110,970	0.4	−0.1
Green	**1**	1	0	+1	285,616	1.0	−0.1
Alliance Party	**1**	1	0	+1	42,762	0.1	+0.0
UKIP	**0**	0	0	0	919,546	3.1	+0.9
BNP	**0**	0	0	0	564,331	1.9	+1.2
Turnout					29,691,380	65.1	+4.0

Table 1.19 Vote share change and net seat change, 1997–2010

Year	Vote share change			Net seat change		
	Con	Lab	Lib Dem	Con	Lab	Lib Dem
1997	−11.3	+9.1	−1.1	−178	+146	+28
2001	+1.2	−2.3	+1.6	+1	−5	+6
2005	+0.5	−5.9	+3.8	+33	−47	+11
2010	+3.7	−6.4	+1.0	+97	−91	−5

Seat changes are adjusted to take account of periodic boundary reviews

Table 1.20 2010 general election results: Scotland

Party	Seats	Gain	Loss	Votes	Vote (%)	+/−
Labour	**41**	0	0	1,035,528	42.0	+2.5
Liberal Democrats	**11**	0	0	465,471	18.9	−3.7
SNP	**6**	0	0	491,386	19.9	+2.3
Conservative	**1**	0	0	412,855	16.7	+0.9
UKIP	**0**	0	0	17,223	0.7	+0.3
Green	**0**	0	0	16,827	0.7	−0.3
BNP	**0**	0	0	8,910	0.4	+0.3
Others	**0**	0	0	17,522	0.7	−0.2
Turnout				2,465,722	63.8	+3.0

Voting behaviour

The study of voting behaviour – the ways in which the public decide which political party to vote for – is a complex issue. Which party an individual votes for is influenced by long-term factors such as social class, gender, age, ethnic and religious background and region; and by short-term factors such as governing competence, the state of the economy and the popularity of the respective parties' leaders and policies.

Political scientists have developed theories of voting behaviour to explain the interaction between the electorate and their voting preferences. They can be divided into long-term and short-term factors.

Long-term factors were considered to be the most important influence on voting behaviour in the period 1945–74. This was an era of party identification, class alignment and two-party dominance. The period between 1979 and the present day is described as one of declining party identification and partisan de-alignment. Short-term factors such as the state of the economy and the image of party leaders are now considered to have a much greater influence on voting behaviour.

Long-term influences

The main theories are the sociological and party identification models, which focus on the social characteristics of voters – especially social class and party loyalties.

Short-term influences

The main theory is the rational choice model, which focuses on the significant issues pertaining to a particular election. In the 2010 general election, the handling of the economic crisis, the competence of Gordon Brown and confidence in the Conservatives to deliver were all key factors (see pages 29–34).

Class voting and partisanship

Until the mid-1970s, social class was regarded as the dominant influence in voting behaviour. P. J. Pulzer, the Oxford political scientist, stated in 1967: 'Class is the basis of British party politics; all else is embellishment and detail.'

Most people voted for the party that best represented the interest of their social group.

A majority of the working class voted for the Labour Party, while much of the middle class supported the Conservatives. Ideologically, Labour was a socialist party. It stood for a redistribution of wealth in society in order to reduce major differences between the rich and poor. Labour believed that large industries, especially utilities like gas and electricity, should be owned by the state. In contrast the Conservatives emphasised less state interference and believed in leaving most economic decision making in the hands of the market economy, while accepting the welfare state including the National Health Service (NHS). The vast majority of the electorate voted either Conservative or Labour: in the 1951 general election 97 per cent of the electorate voted for one of the two main parties. This continuity in voting patterns reflected long-term feelings of positive attachment to one of the main parties (partisanship). This distinct party identification, similar to attachment to a football club, was passed down from generation to generation. However, both class voting and partisanship have declined since the 1970s.

What is social class?

Social class is defined by social and economic status. The working class consists of people in manual occupations and the middle class comprises those in non-manual employment.

The market research definition of class structure uses six categories:

- Categories A, B and C1 are the non-manual middle class.

- Categories C2, D and E constitute the manual working class.

Figure 1.10 A category A worker ↑

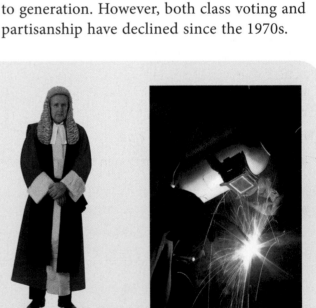

Figure 1.11 A category C2 worker ↑

Partisan de-alignment

The changing trends in social class and voting have been explained by Professor Ivor Crewe (see below). The results of his analysis can be seen in the decline in the number of voters who identified strongly with either Labour or the Conservatives. In 1961 44 per cent of voters were 'very strong' supporters of one of the main parties, but by 2006 this figure had dropped to only 13 per cent. The **core vote** for the two main parties has declined significantly, so political parties now have to work harder to win over **floating voters** who do not have strong allegiances and switch their votes from election to election.

This explains why in the 1980s the Conservatives gained support from the working class. In the 1974 general election only 26 per cent of the skilled working class (C2) voted Conservative; in 1987, 40 per cent voted Conservative. The Conservative government of the 1980s tapped into the aspirations of this new, upwardly mobile, skilled working class through policies such as the sale of council houses, lower taxation and the opportunity for ordinary workers to buy shares in newly privatised industries such as gas and electricity. The expression 'Mondeo man' was later coined to exemplify this new breed of aspiring voter.

New Labour, under the leadership of Tony Blair, was determined to modernise the Labour Party, to end its ties with socialism and reduce its dependence on trade unions. New Labour offered the third way of appealing to all classes and becoming a catch-all party through low taxation, increased NHS spending and attractive social policies such as the introduction of the minimum wage. Labour retained its gains among middle-class

Fact File

The de-alignment explanation

According to Ivor Crewe's analysis of the changing trends in social class and voting, de-alignment means a weakening relationship between social class and party support – a decline in the class basis of UK politics. The distinctions between social classes have been eroded by changes in the labour market, the increase in female and part-time workers, greater affluence and improved access to higher education. Crewe divided the working class into two groups: the old working class and the new working class, who aspire to be middle class.

Features of the old working class:

- unskilled manual occupation in traditional heavy industries
- trade union membership
- living in a council house
- located in greater numbers in the north of England, Wales and Scotland.

Features of the new working class:

- more likely to be skilled, with better qualifications
- owner-occupiers, many having bought their council house under the Conservative policy of right to buy
- working in new high-tech industries
- found in greater numbers in the southern half of England.

voters in 2001 and 2005, but its working-class support fell (see Table 1.21). When he became Conservative leader, David Cameron copied Tony Blair and modernised his party.

It should be emphasised that despite the decline of class voting, it is still an important factor. Labour remains the most popular party among working-class voters and the Conservatives the most popular party among the middle class.

Table 1.21 **Class voting, selected years (share of the vote, %)**

	Middle class (ABC1)	Skilled working class (C2)	Unskilled working class (DE)
Conservative			
1974 (Oct)	56	26	22
1979	59	41	34
1987	54	40	30
1997	39	27	21
2005	37	33	25
2010	39	37	31
Labour			
1974 (Oct)	19	49	57
1979	24	41	49
1987	18	36	48
1997	34	50	59
2005	31	40	48
2010	27	29	40

Table 1.22 **Voting by social class, 2010 general election**

	Conservative	Labour	Liberal Democrats
Overall			
Share of the vote (%)	36.1 (+3.8)	29.0 (−6.2)	23.0 (+1.0)
Seats	307 (+97)	258 (−91)	57 (−5)
By social class (share of the vote, %)			
AB	39 (+2)	27 (−2)	29 (0)
C1	39 (+2)	28 (−4)	24 (+1)
C2	37 (+6)	29 (−11)	22 (0)
DE	31 (+6)	40 (−8)	17 (−1)

Other social factors

Age

There are clear links between age and party support. Labour outperformed the Conservatives among young and middle-aged voters in the four elections prior to the 2010 general election. In contrast, the two older age groups have consistently favoured the Conservatives. In the 2010 general election (see Table 1.23), Labour only outperformed the Conservatives in the 18–24 age group. Interestingly, the largest Liberal Democrat support came from the 18–24 age group (perhaps they were attracted by the party's promise to oppose an increase in student tuition fees!).

Gender

Until the 1997 general election, women were more likely to vote Conservative than men. However, New Labour made significant gains among women under Tony Blair's leadership.

In 2010, women were 5 per cent more likely to vote Conservative than Labour (36 per cent Conservative vs 31 per cent Labour). However, women under the age of 36 were more likely to vote Labour. In contrast, men were 10 per cent more likely to vote Conservative than to vote Labour (38 per cent Conservative vs 28 per cent Labour).

Figure 1.12 Young people casting their votes at the 2010 general election ↑

Table 1.23 Age and voting, 2010 general election

	Conservative	Labour	Liberal Democrats
Overall			
Share of the vote (%)	36.1 (+3.8)	29.0 (−6.2)	23.0 (+1.0)
Seats	307 (+97)	258 (−91)	57 (−5)
By age (share of the vote, %)			
18–24	30 (+2)	31 (−7)	30 (+4)
25–34	35 (+10)	30 (−8)	29 (+2)
35–44	34 (+7)	31 (−10)	26 (+3)
45–54	34 (+3)	28 (−7)	26 (+1)
55–64	38 (−1)	28 (−3)	23 (+1)
65+	44 (+3)	31 (−4)	16 (−2)

Table 1.24 **Gender and voting, 2010 general election**

	Conservative	**Labour**	**Liberal Democrats**
Overall			
Share of the vote (%)	36.1 (+3.8)	29.0 (−6.2)	23.0 (+1.0)
By gender (share of the vote, %)			
Men	38 (+4)	28 (−6)	22 (0)
Women	36 (+4)	31 (−7)	26 (+3)

Ethnicity

Ethnic-minority voters are traditionally far more likely to vote Labour and far less likely to vote Conservative. However, the impact of the Iraq war (short-term influence) contributed to a sharp a drop of 5.5 per cent in support for Labour among Muslim voters. In Bethnal Green in London – a constituency with one of the largest Muslim electorates – George Galloway of the anti-war party Respect defeated the Labour candidate in the 2005 General Election. At the 2010 general election, Labour regained Bethnal Green. The number of ethnic-minority MPs increased after this election, with 27 black and Asian MPs in parliament (16 Labour and 11 Conservative).

Region

There are clear regional variations in voting in Britain. A 'north–south' divide is evident, with Labour support highest in Scotland, Wales, the north of England and large urban areas and council-house schemes; the Conservatives do best in southern England, and in English suburbs and rural areas.

The geographical divisions in voting patterns can be explained in part by social class factors. Labour's safe seats tend to be in inner-city constituencies in cities such as Glasgow and Liverpool. In contrast, Conservative safe seats tend to be in prosperous English constituencies in the suburbs and rural areas. The 2010 general election results make interesting reading (see Table 1.21). Labour experienced a decline in

Figure 1.13 Paul Boateng, Britain's first black cabinet minister ↑

Figure 1.14 Shettleston, in Glasgow's east end ↑

Table 1.25 Regional voting, 2010 general election

	Conservative	Labour	Liberal Democrats
Overall			
Share of the vote (%)	36.1 (+3.8)	29.0 (−6.2)	23.0 (+1.0)
Seats	307 (+97)	258 (−91)	57 (−5)
By region (share of the vote, %)			
The North	24 (+4)	44 (−9)	24 (+0)
Yorkshire and the Humber	33 (+4)	35 (−9)	23 (+2)
North-West	32 (+3)	40 (−6)	22 (+0)
West Midlands	40 (+5)	31 (−8)	21 (+2)
East Midlands	41 (+4)	30 (−9)	21 (+2)
Eastern	47 (+4)	20 (−10)	24 (+2)
London	35 (+3)	37 (−2)	22 (+0)
South-East	50 (+5)	16 (−8)	26 (+1)
South-West	43 (+4)	15 (−7)	35 (+2)
Scotland	18 (+1)	42 (+3)	19 (−4)
Wales	26 (+5)	36 (−7)	20 (+2)

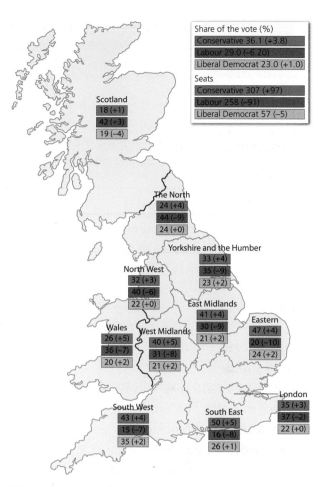

Figure 1.15 % of votes by region in the 2010 general election. The box shows the overall share of the vote and number of seats won by the three main parties ↑

support in its traditional strongholds of Wales and the north of England; however, in Scotland Labour actually increased its support. This may be explained by the loyalty vote to a Scottish prime minister and to Scotland being a more collectivist society, retaining hostile memories of Margaret Thatcher's Conservative Governments of the 1980s and 1990s.

Electoral turnout

The 2010 general election saw turnout increase to 65 per cent, compared to around 60 per cent in the 2001 and 2005 elections. However, it was still way below the post-war average of 78 per cent.

Apathy and disillusionment

It is clear that there is growing dissatisfaction with the political parties and Westminster politics, which has led to a lower turnout. The proportion of the public who have a strong attachment to a political party and who have confidence in politicians has declined. The 2009 MPs' expenses scandal further eroded public confidence and created greater disillusionment.

Critics of first past the post (FPTP) (see page 7) also blame this system as a factor in discouraging turnout.

Social groupings

Clearly, social factors influence turnout. Middle-class, university-educated individuals, older people and those living in rural areas are most likely to vote. People aged over 60 are almost twice as likely to vote as those aged 18–24.

Activities

1 Outline the long-term and short-term explanations of voting behaviour.

2 Why was social class regarded as the most important factor in voting behaviour?

3 Refer to Tables 1.21 and 1.22. What conclusions can be made regarding social class and party support?

4 Explain the term 'partisan de-alignment' and describe its impact on voting behaviour.

5 Assess the influence of other long-term factors on voting behaviour.

Short-term influences

The rational model considers the impact of short-term factors that influence the choice made by individual voters at elections.

Issue voting

All political parties outline their vision for the future and their policies to improve the quality of life of the electorate and their families (see the 2010 UK party manifestos on pages 31–32).

The 1997 general election ended 18 years of Conservative rule and produced a landslide victory for New Labour. Why did the public's perception of how the rival parties would handle decisive issues change after the 1992 general election?

The Conservative image in the period 1979–92 was much more positive than Labour's on party unity, taxation, defence, the economy, and law and order. Moreover, the Conservatives were preferred as the party most likely to offer a strong and capable government.

All this changed with the events of 'Black Wednesday' in September 1992 and the subsequent Conservative disunity on European issues. In September 1992, the Conservative government suffered the humiliation of having to withdraw Britain from the European Exchange Rate Mechanism and to accept the devaluation of the pound. The Conservative Party could no longer claim that the economy was safe in their hands. The disarray over Europe, with Euro-sceptics rebelling in parliament against the passage of the Maastricht Treaty, weakened the Conservative prime minister, John Major.

In contrast, New Labour under Tony Blair and Gordon Brown entered the 1997 general election as a united party with a new vision for Britain. Blair stated that New Labour would establish a third way between the socialism of old Labour and the selfish individualism of Thatcherism. The main issue for the electorate in 1997 was not the respective party policies – it was the record of the Conservative party in office, led by a weak prime minister.

In the 2005 election, Labour was still ahead on the major issues such as the running of the economy; this ensured a return to power, albeit with a reduced majority. Blair's popularity had declined as a result of Britain's involvement in Iraq and the failure to find weapons of mass destruction there.

The 2010 general election

The banking crisis of 2008 and its impact on the world and UK economy would dominate the 2010 election. The greatest challenge facing David Cameron was to convince the electorate that the Conservatives could do a better job than Labour in running the economy and to offer a viable programme of recovery. The age of prosperity had gone and it was clear that financial pain would be the only way to reduce Britain's debt. Labour, on the other hand, highlighted the inexperience of Cameron and his shadow chancellor, George Osborne, and their millionaire background. The Conservatives, aware of the public's strong affection for the NHS, stated that no cuts would be made to the NHS budget and that spending would increase

with inflation. The Conservative strategy was to declare that another five years of Gordon Brown would be a disaster for the UK. Cameron spoke of 'the incredible depression of five more years of Gordon Brown – of a government so dysfunctional and divided, weak, a bunch of ministers who cannot work with him and cannot get rid of him'.

Managing the economy was the most crucial issue for voters. Significantly, 36 per cent of voters believed that no party had the best economic policy. Labour led the Conservatives on health and unemployment, but the Tories were ahead on immigration, crime and defence.

Ipsos/MORI surveys, May 2010

The opinion-poll surveys on the public's perception of the party leaders and their policies indicate why Brown and Labour lost but also why the Conservatives failed to achieve a mandate to govern (see Figures 1.16 and 1.17). The Ipsos/MORI survey clearly identified Cameron as having the most personality of the three leaders and having the best understanding of the problems facing Britain. However, it also identified his lack of experience. Brown was identified as having the most experience

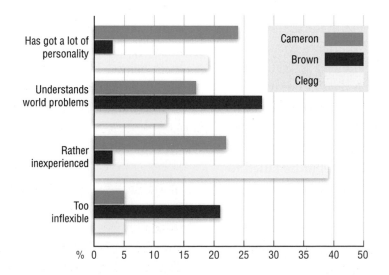

Figure 1.16 Positive and negative attributes of the party leaders (source: Ipsos/MORI, May 2010) ↑

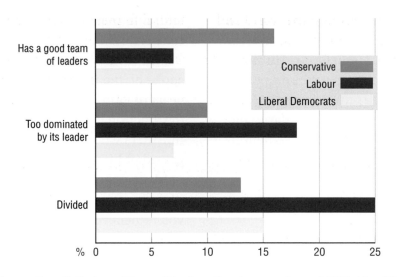

Figure 1.17 Positive and negative attributes of the political parties (source: Ipsos/MORI, May 2010) ↑

and the best understanding of world problems. However Brown's perceived inflexibility and lack of personality perhaps explain why the electorate deserted Labour. Campaign events such as Brown's meeting with Gillian Duffy would have reinforced this negative image. Clegg came across as the most honest but also the most inexperienced. High approval ratings for Clegg did not translate into votes.

What really sank Labour was the public's perception of them as a divided, faction-ridden party. Some Blair loyalists seemed determined to prevent Brown from winning the election – three attempted coups were made against his leadership. They seemed prepared to accept a Conservative government as a price worth paying. In contrast, the Conservatives were seen as having the best leaders and being a more united party. Cameron had neutralised the negative image that his party had in previous elections (except in Scotland), but he failed to 'seal the deal' with the electorate.

Bigotgate

The defining moment of the 2010 campaign was Gordon Brown's self-inflicted disaster during his meeting with Gillian Duffy, a 65-year-old pensioner, in the marginal constituency of Rochdale. In his televised conversation with Mrs Duffy they discussed her concern over the number of immigrants in the local area. Unfortunately for the prime minister, he committed the cardinal sin of all politicians – making indiscreet comments while the microphone was still live and attached to his lapel. Once he was back in his official car, Brown was in a foul mood and attacked Gillian Duffy: 'She [Mrs Duffy] was just a sort of bigoted woman who said she used to be Labour. I mean it's just ridiculous.' Every word that he said was being transmitted from his microphone and was being recorded by a nearby Sky News satellite truck.

Figure 1.18 Gordon Brown's conversation with Gillian Duffy was this election's defining moment ↑

This gaffe was beamed around the world and was the leading story in all the British television and radio news programmes. Brown immediately apologised for calling her a racist; however, his humiliation was compounded by Mrs Duffy's refusal to meet him for a photograph together at her front door after he went to apologise four hours later. The Tory press had a field day and savaged Brown in the following day's newspapers.

Activities

1 Outline the main short-term factors that enabled Labour to win the 1997 and 2005 general elections.

2 What were the main issues of the 2010 general election and why was so much coverage given to Gordon Brown's meeting with Mrs Duffy?

3 Refer to the Ipsos/MORI opinion polls and compare the public's perception of the three main parties and their leaders. What light do they shed on why the Conservatives failed to achieve a winning majority?

4 Why would the findings of these opinion polls not apply to Scotland?

5 Refer to the summaries of the parties' manifestos (Table 1.26). To what extent are the policies of Labour and the Conservatives similar, and are the Liberal Democrats' policies different?

Table 1.26 **Selected policies from the 2010 party manifestos**

Policy area	Conservative	Labour	Liberal Democrats
Economic policy	Emergency budget within 50 days. Up to £6 billion in public-spending cuts in first year. Cuts in corporation tax and National Insurance. Freeze on council tax. 'No' to the euro.	No major cuts in first year. Sale of nationalised banks. No increase in income tax. A referendum before any decision to join the euro.	No major cuts in first year. No income tax on first £10,000. 'Mansion tax' on properties over £2 million. Close tax loopholes. Break up banks. Favour joining the euro, but only after a referendum.
Home affairs	Scrap ID-cards scheme. 'Grounding orders' for anti-social behaviour. Annual cap on immigration. Prison sentence for those carrying knives.	Maintain police numbers. Successful police forces take over failing ones. Points-based system to limit immigration. More prison places.	Scrap ID-cards scheme. 'Amnesty' for most long-term illegal immigrants. 30,000 more police officers. Stop building new prisons. Regional, points-based immigration system.

Policy area	Conservative	Labour	Liberal Democrats
Social policy	Tax breaks for married couples on low to middle incomes. Remove tax credits for households earning more than £50,000. Form of national service for 16-year-olds. Neighbourhood groups to take over badly performing public services.	Protect Sure Start centre budgets. 15 hours' free nursery provision for 3–5-year-olds. Enhanced paternity leave. Restore link between state pension and average earnings from 2012.	Shared parental leave extended to 18 months. Access to 20 hours of free childcare from the age of 18 months. Scrap compulsory retirement ages and restore link between state pension and average earnings.
Foreign policy and security	Replace Trident missile system. Establish US-style National Security Council.	Maintain nuclear deterrent and build two new aircraft carriers. Give aid to failing states. Regulate the arms trade.	No direct replacement for Trident. Regulate arms exports. Inquiry into UK involvement in torture.
Constitutional reform	Cut the number of MPs. Equalise the size of constituency electorates. Allow recall of MPs in cases of serious wrongdoing. Parliamentary debate for any public petition gaining 100,000 signatures. Prevent former ministers taking up lobbying posts within 2 years. Replace the Human Rights Act with a British Bill of Rights.	Recall of MPs. Referendum on moving to the alternative vote (AV) system for elections to Westminster. Referendum on Lords reform. Greater power for local government. Fixed-term parliaments. Register of lobbyists. Votes for 16-year-olds.	Cut the number of MPs. Recall of MPs. Freedom Bill to regulate CCTV and protect the Human Rights Act. Proportional representation system for elections to Westminster. Fully elected second chamber. Greater power for local government. Fixed-term parliaments. Votes for 16-year-olds.

The media and elections

A distinction is now made between the old media (television and radio) and the new media of social networking sites such as Facebook and Twitter. In the 2008 US presidential election, Barack Obama and his supporters used social networking sites with a devastating effect to build a campaign that reached way beyond the party faithful. Obama's My Vote website attracted 20 million supporters who provided grass-roots and financial support for the Democratic campaign. It was expected that the new media would dominate the UK 2010 general election. Gordon Brown's wife, Sarah Brown, skilfully used social networking sites to present herself as the first lady of British politics, thus emulating Michelle Obama. Her Twitter page, set up in March 2009 to describe life in Downing Street, had a following of over a million readers by March 2010. She used this site to present the human face of her husband and to detoxify the negative image of Gordon Brown.

Yet it was the old media that shaped and transformed the campaigning process. The televised debates between the three leaders made television king and provided Nick Clegg with the opportunity to undermine the dominance of the two-party system.

Figure 1.19 The 2010 leaders' debates ↑

Thanks to television, the contest became a genuine three-horse race that would transform the direction of post-war elections. The new media provided instant feedback on each debate and the newspapers, through their commissioning of political surveys, provided instant assessment of the performance of the three leaders.

The televised debates

For the first time ever, the two major parties agreed to hold televised debates between their leaders; to the surprise of many, they agreed to include the Liberal Democrats' leader, Nick Clegg. Both the SNP and Plaid Cymru were unhappy with this proposal and threatened to take legal action. In Scotland the SNP eventually, and with reluctance, accepted a separate leaders' debate between the Scottish parties.

The first debate was a triumph for Clegg. While Brown was dour and Cameron too slick and nervous, Clegg was a natural on television. This debate suddenly turned the election into a genuine three-horse race. Within days, the Liberal Democrats' projected share of the vote had risen by about 11 points – the highest increase ever recorded during an election campaign. Two opinion polls placed the Liberal Democrats ahead of both the Conservatives and Labour for the first time in over 100 years.

The Tory press switched their guns to attack the Liberal Democrats and to character-assassinate Nick Clegg, while continuing their brutal attacks on Brown (see pages 34–36).

The *Mail on Sunday* declared: 'His [Clegg's] wife is Spanish, his mother Dutch, his father is half-Russian and his spin doctor German. Is there anything BRITISH about the Lib Dem leader?'

A 76-point agreement underpinned the three 30-minute debates. Brown declined the option of being in the middle and was placed on the right of the camera to accommodate his poor eyesight.

Viewing figures

- First debate (ITV): 9.9 million.

- Second debate (Sky News): 4 million.

- Third debate (BBC): 8.4 million.

Key phrases of the debates

- Nick Clegg: 'The more they attack each other, the more they seem the same.'

- 'I agree with Nick' – used by Gordon Brown seven times in the first debate.

Nicholas Jones (political journalist): 'In the final stages of the election campaign, the fawning of the Tory press in their coverage of Cameron was matched only by the brutality of their treatment of Gordon Brown and their savage character assassination of Clegg.'

Do newspapers influence the outcome of elections?

Ever since *The Sun*'s 1992 notorious front-page headline 'It's the Sun wot won it', claiming credit for the Conservatives' victory, there has been an ongoing debate between academics and political strategists about the extent to which any one paper can influence voters. John Curtice, professor of politics at Strathclyde University, argues that there is no evidence to support the view that newspaper endorsement affects elections and that the 'aggregate effect of newspapers' influence approximates to zero'. The Scottish Parliament elections are a case in point. In 2007 the two best-selling newspapers in Scotland, the *Daily Record* and *The Sun*, supported Labour and were hostile to the SNP yet the SNP won the election and formed a minority government. An alternative argument might be that if these newspapers had supported the SNP (as *The Sun* did in 2011), then they might have had a greater number of MSPs.

What is clear is that politicians and their spin doctors dearly wish to have the support of the best-selling newspapers. Neil Kinnock, the former Labour leader, is convinced to this day that *The Sun*'s vicious anti-Labour campaign enabled the Conservatives to win the 1992 election. Martin Linton, author of *Was It the Sun Wot Won It?*, argues that *The Sun*'s character assassination of Kinnock and fabrication of Labour policies enabled John Major to retain about 30 marginal seats. Linton stated: 'Readers of *The Sun* and *The Mirror* are from the same social group but *The Sun*'s readers are less committed to a party, less interested in politics, so more easily influenced by attacks on character and distortion.'

As Table 1.27 confirms, up to 1997 the British press was predominantly Conservative in its political support. At the time of the 1992 general election there were 8.7 million readers of newspapers favouring the Conservatives to 3.3 million readers of pro-Labour papers. New Labour under Blair shook off its socialist beliefs and entered the 1997 election as a united party: in contrast, the Tories were divided. Blair's meetings with Rupert Murdoch paid off, and in 1997 *The Sun* switched to Labour, claiming it was the natural party of government. Murdoch's News International continued to support Labour in the 2001 and 2005 elections. Murdoch's four titles – *The Times*, *Sunday Times*, *The Sun* and *News of the World* – represented 42 per cent of the national newspaper market, which explains why politicians are so eager for Murdoch's support.

As the Conservative Party leader, David Cameron set out to try and gain Murdoch's support. In January 2007 Andy Coulson resigned as editor of the *News of the World*, after his reporters were found guilty of forming part of a conspiracy that used criminal methods to access the voicemail of members of the royal family, among others. Four months later, Cameron appointed the disgraced former editor as the

Table 1.27 Ownership and political allegiance of major British newspapers

Newspaper	Circulation (Aug 2010)	Party preferences and/or endorsements				
		1992	1997	2001	2005	2010
Daily Mail	2,129,278	Con	Con	Con	Con	Con
Daily Express	642,491	Con	Con	Lab	Con	Con
Mirror	1,282,290	Lab	Lab	Lab	Lab	Lab
Sun	2,904,000	Con	Lab	Lab	Lab	Con
Independent	182,412	None	Lab	Lab	Lab + more Lib Dem	Labour + Lib Dem
Times	480,000	Con	None	Lab	Lab	Con
Financial Times	401,898	None	None	Lab	Lab	Con
Telegraph	655,664	Con	Con	Con	Con	Con
Guardian	276,428	Lab	Lab	Lab	Lab + more Lib Dem	Lib Dem

Conservative Party's director of communications. (Coulson resigned from this post in January 2011 after new allegations were made about phone hacking by the *News of the World*.) Cameron further endeared himself to Murdoch in 2009 with his attack on a bloated BBC and a promise that a new Conservative Government would open up the digital and online market to the benefit of the commercial sector.

On 30 September 2009, the morning after Gordon Brown's speech to the Labour Party conference, *The Sun* switched back to the Conservatives. 'Labour's lost it', declared its banner headlines (see Figure 1.20). The vilification of Brown and Labour had begun (see 'Suntalk', page 36).

Figure 1.20 Front pages of *The Sun* in 1997 and 2010 ↑

Suntalk

Comments on the September 2010 Labour conference

'I want someone to pass the sick bucket when Sarah Brown said her hero was Gordon Brown … He ruined the country … We say David Cameron should be next prime minister … Brown is dead.'

Declaring war on Murdoch

Until the early 1990s, British television was dominated by the terrestrial channels of the British Broadcasting Corporation (BBC) and Independent Television (ITV). The emergence of satellite and cable television has challenged their monopoly of news delivery. The growth of Sky News was reflected in its involvement in the 2010 leadership debates.

The growing influence of Rupert Murdoch is a concern for many, particularly with his £8 billion bid to gain complete control of BSkyB. In December 2010, the Liberal Democrat cabinet minister Vince Cable was revealed by the *Daily Telegraph* to have 'declared war on Murdoch'.

Unfortunately for Cable, he should have been impartial because he was part of the government group that would decide on Murdoch's bid. Humiliated, Cable was demoted and removed from any decision-making role.

The demise of Murdoch and News International?

The investigation into phone hacking by the *News of the World* led to the discovery that the tabloid had hacked into the voicemail of a missing schoolgirl, Milly Dowler, who was later found murdered. The public were horrified by this revelation and prominent brands withdrew their advertising from the newspaper. A week later, on 10 July 2011, the *News of the World* closed down. Rupert Murdoch's News Corporation also withdrew its controversial bid to take full control of BSkyB – Britain's largest satellite television broadcaster. In the same month Andy Coulson was arrested and questioned by police over the phone hacking claims and reports that he had authorised *News of the World* journalists to pay police officers for information. This revelation was damaging for the Prime Minister, David Cameron, due to his appointment of Coulson as his Director of Communications.

Television

Unlike newspapers, television stations are expected not to favour a particular political party and instead to display balance. But obviously the party political broadcasts, usually transmitted before elections, are partisan. The time allocated to the political parties during a UK general election is based on their representation at Westminster, and this favours the Conservatives and Labour.

The BBC came into conflict with the Labour government over its reporting of the Iraq war and the issue of weapons of mass destruction. A BBC reporter, Andrew Gilligan, claimed on Radio 4's *The Today Programme* that the government had exaggerated the evidence to support the claim of Iraq having such weapons.

Dr David Kelly, thought to be Gilligan's source, committed suicide shortly after appearing before the Commons Select Committee on Foreign Affairs. In July 2003, the Blair government appointed Lord Hutton to conduct an inquiry into Dr Kelly's death.

In January 2004, the Hutton Report's conclusions were largely favourable to the government and highly critical of the BBC. This led to a major shake-up in the BBC, with among others the director general, Greg Dyke, resigning.

Supporters of the BBC claimed the report was a 'whitewash', and Dyke himself accused the government of systematic bullying of the BBC over coverage of the Iraq war.

It was expected that the digital explosion in social networking sites would diminish the influence of traditional media (television and radio) during the 2010 general election. However, this was not the case: it was television, through the leaders' debates, that was the dominant factor.

Nicholas Jones summed up the media's influence: 'The digital election campaign remained the preserve of a relatively small percentage of the total electorate and the consistent verdict of opinion polls was that for a high proportion of voters the television debates had by far the greatest impact.'

Fact File

Referenda

A referendum is a ballot in which the voters, not their representatives in parliament, pass judgement on a particular issue. They are not held often in Britain but are common in other countries such as the USA. It is a form of direct democracy because it involves citizens directly in decision making. A referendum can be useful for overcoming divisions within a government.

Many within the Conservative Party wish to keep the present FPTP system and so, rather than passing legislation to introduce AV, David Cameron agreed to leave this decision to the electorate.

The only other national referendum was held by Labour in 1975 on continued membership of the European Union, because the party was divided over this issue. Referenda have been held to establish a devolved government in Scotland and a devolved assembly in Wales. In November 2004, a resounding 'no' vote ended Labour's plan for a regional assembly in the North-East of England.

Opponents of referenda argue that it undermines the UK system of representative democracy, undermines parliamentary sovereignty and can enable pressure groups to influence the outcome.

Activities

1   What evidence suggests that newspapers influence voting behaviour?

2   Why do television and radio stations provide balanced coverage of elections?

3   Assess the impact of the televised debates on the outcome of the 2010 general election.

4   Refer to Table 1.27. What conclusions can you draw about newspapers' changing support of political parties?

5   Outline the arguments for and against referenda.

Essay questions

1   Short-term influences on voting behaviour now have a greater impact than long-term influences. Discuss.

2   Critically examine the influence of social class on voting behaviour.

3   To what extent is the media the most important influence on voting behaviour?

2 Decision making in central government

Parliament

Parliament is the highest legislative authority in the UK, giving it supreme law-making power. It also carries the responsibility of scrutinising (or checking on) the work of the government. The UK Parliament is made up of three parts: the House of Commons, the House of Lords and the monarch (the King or Queen). All three institutions combine to carry out the work of parliament.

However, the legislature in the UK is bicameral. This means that legislative business takes place in two chambers or houses – the House of Commons and the House of Lords. The House of Commons is known as the lower house and, despite its name, is the dominant chamber. The House of Lords is known as the upper house. We elect 650 MPs to the House of Commons, and about 780 peers have the right to sit in the House of Lords.

Parliament and the constitution

What gives parliament this supreme legal authority is what is called parliamentary sovereignty; in other words, parliament is the sovereign body in the UK and is a principle of the UK constitution. The UK's constitution is often thought of as being unwritten. While it does not exist as a single written document (as in the USA), much of the UK constitution is in fact written down in the form of laws passed by parliament that are known as statute law. The constitution is better referred to as being uncodified, meaning that the UK does not have a single, written constitution. Several recently passed laws have placed serious limits on parliamentary sovereignty, but these do not

Figure 2.1 The state opening of parliament ↑

38

ultimately undermine the principle – because parliament could repeal any of them.

Laws affecting parliamentary sovereignty

- The establishment of a UK Supreme Court in 2009, which ended the House of Lords' function as the UK's final court of appeal.

- The devolution of power to the Scottish Parliament and Welsh Assembly.

- The Human Rights Act (1998).

- The UK's entry to the European Union in 1972.

Parliamentary business is carried out in both the House of Commons and the House of Lords. The work of each house is similar: making laws (legislation), checking the work of the Government (scrutiny) and debating current issues. Generally, the decisions made in one house have to be approved by the other. In this way the two-chamber system acts as a check and balance for both houses. MPs sit in the House of Commons and are publicly elected. The membership of the House of Lords is mostly appointed and includes experts from many fields.

Constitutional monarchy

In the past, the monarchy was very powerful but over time its powers have been given over to parliament because of social and political changes. Today, the UK's parliamentary system includes a constitutional monarchy that is hereditary. While the monarch is the head of state, he or she has no effective political power but does serve a more traditional and ceremonial function in parliament.

Prerogative powers

The power of the monarch to act without first consulting parliament is known as the royal prerogative. Whereas in the past the monarch was able to do this, today these powers are exercised through the prime minister and his or her government.

The royal assent

Before a bill can become law it must be signed by the monarch. Constitutional convention requires that the monarch must give his or her approval; the royal assent has not been refused since 1707.

Appointing the prime minister

The monarch appoints the prime minister and other ministers of the crown. This is a formality because each political party has its own method of electing its leader. After a general election, the leader of the largest party in the House of Commons is expected to be invited to become prime minister and form a government. Other ministers are chosen by the prime minister, who will discuss their choices with the monarch.

Dissolution of parliament

Before parliament can be dissolved and a general election called, the prime minister must ask for the monarch's permission. Again, this is a formality and is carried out on the advice of the prime minister.

Figure 2.2 The Queen's speech marks the beginning of the parliamentary year ←

State opening of parliament and the Queen's speech

Parliament decides when the parliamentary year will start and end; the monarch simply has a ceremonial role in opening and closing it. The reading of the Queen's speech by the monarch at the state opening of parliament marks the beginning of the parliamentary year. This speech lays out the main bills that the government will introduce in the coming year; it is actually written by the prime minister and his or her officials.

House of Commons

As the dominant chamber in parliament, the House of Commons has several key roles or functions. The most important are:

- legislation
- scrutiny
- representation.

Legislation

The primary function of parliament is to make laws and change existing laws. However, a new law must pass through and complete a series of stages in both the House of Commons and the House of Lords, with mutual agreement by both. A bill, which can begin in either house, is a proposal for a new law or a proposal to change an existing law that is debated in parliament. Either house can vote down a bill, in which case it will normally not become law – but there are exceptions. The Commons can pass the same bill in two successive years, in which case it can become law without the agreement of the Lords. Bills that are only about money (raising taxes or authorising government expenditure) are not opposed in the Lords and may only be delayed for a month. The monarch must then also give it the royal assent (or approval) by signing it. At this point, the bill becomes an Act of Parliament and is a law.

The process by which a bill becomes a law is characterised by a series of debates, scrutiny and amendment. The complete process is explained below.

White paper: This contains the government's idea for a bill. It is written to allow discussion and consultation with interested parties before the idea becomes a bill.

First reading: The bill is read to or introduced to parliament without a debate or vote taking place.

Second reading: The bill is debated and must be approved in a vote to proceed.

Committee stage: The bill goes through detailed scrutiny by an all-party Public Bill Committee and amendments are made, if required.

Report stage: The whole House of Commons considers any amendments made by the Committee and can accept, alter or reject them.

Third reading: The amended bill is debated but cannot be amended again at this stage. A vote is taken on whether to accept the amended bill.

If the amended bill passes this stage it goes to the House of Lords, where the whole process is repeated. If the Lords amend the bill even more, it is returned to the Commons for approval; at this point, the amendments made by the Lords may be accepted, rejected or changed by the House of Commons. This can lead to what is known as 'parliamentary ping-pong', as a bill is bounced back and forth between the two houses. Ultimately though, if agreement cannot be reached it is the Commons that has the upper hand. It can accept the Lords' amendments, drop the bill altogether or invoke the Parliament Act.

The two most important stages in the passage of a bill are the second reading and the committee stage. During the second reading, the principle of the bill is debated and at this stage it is vulnerable to being thrown out after a vote by the house. At the committee stage, the Public Bill Committee – which is made up of a majority of government MPs and may include party whips – can usually ensure a safe passage for the bill. They can ensure that strong party discipline helps to speed up this stage and that their majority prevents any unwelcome amendments from opposition MPs by voting against them. This ability to prevent opposition amendments at the committee stage has led to criticisms that the ability of backbench MPs to scrutinise is minimal, because as long as the government has a majority it is easy for it to do what it wants regardless of opposition. After the 2010 general election, the coalition government had a working majority of 84.

Government and private members' bills

Government bills usually affect the general public and are sponsored and supported by a government minister. This gives the bill a higher chance of becoming an Act of Parliament because of the government majority in the House of Commons. A current government bill is the Grandparents (Access Rights) Bill (2010–11). This is a bill to give grandparents rights of access to their grandchildren in certain circumstances.

Table 2.1 clearly shows the success rate of government bills and the lack of success of private members' bills. It is interesting to note that with its large majority Labour was able to pass all government bills between its election in 1997 and 2005, when it suffered a defeat at the second stage of its Terrorism Bill.

On the other hand, backbench MPs of the governing party are more likely to influence the government's decision making during this process than opposition backbenchers. This is because the government majority on the committee does not need the support of the opposition members to drive forward its legislation, but it does need the support of its own backbench members. Any potential dissent or rebellion from its own backbenchers will make the government listen and agree to amend legislation. However, it is likely that any such amendments will be agreed before the bill is presented for its first reading.

Scrutiny

The House of Commons has a duty to scrutinise (or examine and challenge) the work of the government on behalf of the public to ensure accountability. MPs have the power to force

Table 2.1 Success rates of government bills and private members' bills, 2007–10

	Parliamentary session	Number introduced	Number successful
Government bills	2009–10	23	23
	2008–9	26	25
	2007–8	32	32
Private members' bills	2009–10	67	7
	2008–9	112	5
	2007–8	100	3

Source: www.parliament.uk (Commons Seasonal Information Digests)

the government and ministers to justify and explain their policies and actions, and even to dismiss the government. The main way they scrutinise is through questioning government ministers, debating current issues and policy and the investigative work of committees. The government can publicly respond to explain and justify its policies and decisions.

Questions

MPs can ask questions of government ministers. The majority of questions asked receive written answers, but some are answered orally for around an hour each day from Monday to Thursday on the floor of the house. The prime minister answers questions each Wednesday at noon for 30 minutes. These sessions provide an opportunity for the leader of the opposition and backbench MPs (selected by the speaker) to 'grill' the prime minister or minister about their policies or actions. Most of the questions are passed on to MPs by the whips; however, a backbench MP could use question time as an opportunity to ask a question about their constituency. The high-drama event is prime minister's question time, when the leader of the opposition will try to embarrass the prime minister or government by exposing a policy failure. Overall, the restrictive nature of question

Figure 2.3 Prime minister's question time ↑

time limits the effectiveness of this as a means of scrutiny.

Debates

At the end of each day's business, the house adjourns or suspends proceedings until the following day's sitting with a half-hour adjournment debate. This gives MPs an opportunity to discuss government policy, proposed new laws and current issues, but also to raise issues of concern and interest to their constituents. These debates are designed to help MPs reach an informed decision on a subject but are often poorly attended. Since 1999, 'Westminster Hall' debates have taken place to allow MPs more time to debate big issues.

Parliamentary committees

In 2010, the ability of parliament and backbench MPs to effectively scrutinise the decision-making process was enhanced. Following a report by the Select Committee on Reform of the House of Commons, the independence of Commons select committees was strengthened by two important changes. Firstly, chairs are now elected on a free and secret ballot of all MPs; secondly, backbench members – not whips – determine who should represent their party on each committee. As a result of these two changes, the effectiveness of select committees to scrutinise has been enhanced, with some now arguing that the House of Commons has a means of impartial, systematic scrutiny of the government that can be much more rigorous than debates and questions. Members can now be critics rather than party loyalists. However, others

> David Cameron, May 2009: 'There are far too many laws being pushed through, with far too little genuine scrutiny from MPs. And excessive "whipping" of MPs by party hierarchies further limits genuine scrutiny. This, too, has to change.'

argue that David Cameron's reforms to improve parliament's scrutiny powers are a sham (see '"New politics" claim is a sham', below).

'New politics' claim is a sham, warns top Tory

A senior Tory MP has launched a stinging attack on David Cameron and party whips after a fellow Conservative, Dr Sarah Wollaston – who worked for 24 years as a doctor – complained that she had been told 'to say nothing and vote with the government over its controversial health reforms'. Bernard Jenkin, Chairman of the Commons Public Administration Select Committee, said that 'the way the whips are operating at present makes a complete nonsense of David Cameron's pledge before the election about strengthening parliament and improving scrutiny of legislation and the executive.' He also stated that selection for standing committees should no longer be left up to 'stooges and whips'.

Figure 2.4 Bernard Jenkin MP ↑

Commons select committees

Government departmental select committees in the House of Commons scrutinise the work of all major government departments and concentrate on expenditure, policies and administration. They are the most effective means of parliamentary scrutiny of the executive and the decision-making process. Select committees have eleven backbench MP members who are elected by their own party members; previously, members were selected by party whips (hence the name 'select committee'). Each party is represented in proportion to the number of MPs it has in the House of Commons. The committees gather written evidence and examine witnesses, then report their findings and recommendations to the Commons. The government must respond to all reports and usually has 60 days to do so.

There are nineteen departmental select committees, one to shadow each department of state, and several that look at a particular issue across departments – such as the Public Accounts, Public Administration, Environmental Audit and European Scrutiny committees.

Their powers derive from the House of Commons itself and include the ability to meet outside Westminster, meet with other committees, appoint outside specialist advisers, and send for 'people, papers and records'. This means that if a witness is unwilling to give evidence, the committee can serve them with an order to attend or produce papers or records. The select committee system allows for the questioning of ministers and forces them to explain themselves.

Following the announcement by the chancellor in his 2010 Budget not to proceed with the proposed tax relief for the video games industry, the Scottish Affairs Select Committee undertook an inquiry into the impact of this decision on the video games industry in Scotland and to examine alternative financial incentives for the industry. The committee members went to Dundee, visiting the University of Abertay and two video games studios, as well as holding a round-table discussion with representatives from the industry. They requested written evidence and called forward witnesses to provide oral evidence: representatives of trade associations, the University of Abertay, HM Treasury and Ed Vaizey MP, Minister for Culture, Communications and the Creative Industries.

Case Study: Cross-party select committee

In 2010, the Commons Committee of Public Accounts published a report on the major projects of the Ministry of Defence (MOD). Margaret Hodge MP, chair of the committee, criticised the government and the MOD by stating in her report that poor decisions had led to billions of pounds being wasted with additional costs being met by taxpayers. She called on them to spell out how they were going to get their defence procurement budget under control.

Criticism of select committees

Because select committee membership reflects the composition of the House of Commons, a government with a majority in the house also has a majority on committees. This means that most committee members are also members of the same governing party, and this presents them with the problem of scrutinising too vigorously in public. Just how can a career-minded backbench MP from the governing party who is a select committee member effectively scrutinise a government department in public alongside opposition backbenchers? They may be reluctant to expose malpractice or irregularities in the government of which they wish to be a part.

Also, witnesses can withhold important information. For example, when the Foreign Affairs Select Committee scrutinised the issues surrounding the Iraq war, evidence was routinely withheld on the grounds that it would compromise national security and undermine the work of the intelligence services.

Furthermore, the government is not bound by any recommendations made by select committees, and after giving its response to any recommendations it can simply reject them.

Public bills committees

In 2006, public bills committees were introduced in place of standing committees to scrutinise legislation. Unlike standing committees, they act in a similar way to select committees: they can call forward witnesses to obtain evidence on the bills and request written information from any interested parties and thereby add teeth to their legislative scrutiny and its potential impact. However, their composition still reflects the proportion of the parties in parliament, meaning that the government retains a majority on each committee – easing the passage of bills.

Backbench business committee

This is a fairly new development, giving backbench MPs the power to call for debates in the chamber and in Westminster Hall at least once a week. However, the current committee consists of only eight MPs – four Conservative, three Labour and one Liberal Democrat – leading to the criticism that smaller parties are being excluded.

Figure 2.5 Tony Blair giving evidence to the Foreign Affairs Select Committee on the Iraq war ↑

Representation

Members of Parliament

Each MP is elected from a single-member constituency and is expected to represent their constituents. However, in most cases they are also members of a party and so are expected to support their party leader. This can cause conflict at times. Most MPs are backbenchers, and those of the governing party are expected to

Fact File

Our MPs

Educational background

- 90 per cent went to university; 25 per cent attended Oxford or Cambridge.

- Almost one in three Conservatives went to Oxford or Cambridge.

- 35 per cent attended private school (more than 50 per cent of Conservatives and 41 per cent of Liberal Democrats), compared to 7 per cent of the national population.

- Nineteen Conservatives and one Liberal Democrat went to Eton College.

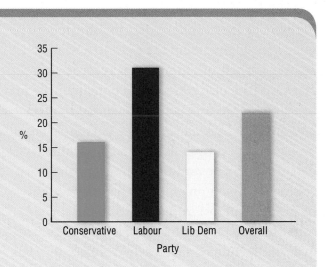

Figure 2.6 The percentage of female MPs ↑

Vocational background

- 48 per cent come from only three professions: business, finance and law.

- 27 per cent of Conservatives have worked in finance compared to only 3 per cent of Labour MPs.

- More Labour MPs have worked in the public and voluntary sector.

Gender

- There are 504 male and 144 female MPs.

- 51 per cent of the UK's population is female.

- 22 per cent of MPs in the current parliament are female – the highest percentage ever.

Ethnicity

- Twenty-seven MPs (4.1 per cent) are from an ethnic minority, up from fourteen in 2005 – but 8 per cent of the population has an ethnic-minority background.

- The Conservatives have eleven non-white MPs, compared to two in the last parliament.

- Helen Grant is Britain's first black female Conservative MP.

- Britain's first three female Muslim MPs all represent Labour.

Age

- The oldest MP is Sir Peter Tapsell, Conservative MP for Louth and Horncastle, aged 80.

- The youngest MP is Pamela Nash, Labour MP for Airdrie and Shotts, aged 25.

- The average age of an MP is 50.

The information in this Fact File is accurate as of September 2011.

support the government and not be too vigorous in their criticisms – especially when there is a conflict of interest between the government's policy and the interests of their constituents or constituency. Nevertheless, backbench MPs have many opportunities to influence the decision-making process. At the start of each day in parliament they can take part in ministers' questions, giving them the right to a written answer to their question that is recorded in Hansard (the official report of parliament) – and so can be more useful and influential than an oral answer. They can also take part in debates on legislation proposals and in adjournment debates with a government minister, who must respond to them on an issue that may well be of specific interest to their constituents. They can also take part in and have a level of control over the agenda of debates in Westminster Hall. Finally, they can take part in committee work and introduce a private members' bill if they are successful in the ballot.

Since the 2010 general election, MPs are more likely to have been educated at independent schools and come from a business background, leading to claims that parliament is becoming 'less representative'. Nevertheless, there has been a greater overall increase in female MPs than at any other time, along with a record rise in those from black and ethnic-minority groups. Labour returned three female Muslim MPs – the first Muslim women elected to parliament – and the Conservatives now have their first black female MP.

Educational background of MPs in 2011

An analysis by the Sutton Trust charity shows that more than a third (35 per cent) of MPs attended fee-paying schools, even though these schools educate just 7 per cent of the population. It was the highest rate since 1992 and up on the 32 per cent of MPs elected in 2005. The charity said numbers were fuelled by a rise in Conservative MPs, who are much more likely to be privately educated than those from Labour. The report revealed that 20 MPs, including David Cameron and Zac Goldsmith, were educated at Eton College, compared with 15 five years ago. Two independent schools – Highgate in north London and Millfield in Somerset – accounted for five MPs each, while Westminster and Nottingham High had four. Less than half of MPs were educated at state comprehensives, with 22 per cent from grammar schools. The study also found that almost a third of MPs were Oxford or Cambridge graduates, although numbers have fallen since a high in the 1960s and 1970s.

Occupation, gender and ethnic origin of MPs in 2011

An analysis from the Smith Institute found that politicians were much more likely to come from business backgrounds or professions such as the law, media and public affairs than the general public. Around 27 per cent of Conservative MPs have worked in finance, compared with just 3 per cent of Labour MPs.

But figures show that the Conservatives have taken huge strides towards gender balance. A record 22 per cent of all MPs are now women, almost four times the number elected in 1987. The Conservative Party almost doubled its number of female MPs at the 2010 election, and the proportion soared from 9 to 17 per cent.

Figure 2.7 Shabana Mahmood, one of Britain's first Muslim female MPs ←

More people from black and ethnic minority backgrounds were elected in 2010, with numbers almost doubling from 14 to 27. Labour MPs Rushanara Ali (Bethnal Green and Bow), Yasmin Qureshi (Bolton South East) and Shabana Mahmood (Birmingham Ladywood) became the first Muslim women to sit in Westminster. Helen Grant became the first black woman to represent the Conservatives after retaining Ann Widdecombe's safe seat of Maidstone and the Weald.

Whips and party discipline

Ultimately, backbench MPs can rebel and break party unity. It is the job of party whips to enforce strong party discipline. They are MPs appointed by each party to help make sure that the maximum number of their party members vote, and vote the way their party wants. The party whip ensures that MPs toe the party line and drives rebellious or straying MPs back into line with the party. Whips also act as tellers by counting votes in divisions and organising the pairing system, whereby pairs of opposing MPs both agree not to vote when either is prevented from being at Westminster.

The big dilemma for MPs arises when there is a conflict of interest. Is the MP solely the representative of their constituents, or a loyal supporter of the party? Are they free to vote in the interest of their constituents or constituency, or are they bound to follow instructions from their party? In most cases, MPs do as their party wishes and vote when and as instructed by the whips. Loyalty and toeing the party line can lead to reward and promotion, whereas disloyalty can lead to sanctions and ultimately removal from the party – bringing an end to a career. This is what happened to former Labour MP Ken Livingstone, who was thrown out of the party.

The job of the whips becomes more important if the majority of the party in government is small or (as was the case after the 2010 election) when a coalition is formed, because this can make it more likely that the government lose major votes. Therefore, it is crucial that both government and opposition whips get as many of their MPs to vote as possible, and with their party.

From the setting up of Cameron's coalition government in May 2010 until February 2011, there were more rebellions than the Blair government suffered in its whole first term from 1997 to 2001. The total reached 97 in the first nine months, when in February 2011 both Conservative and Liberal Democrat MPs rebelled over plans to sell off Britain's forests to private companies; there were only 96 rebellions among Labour MPs between 1997 and 2001.

The Centre for British Politics at Nottingham University pointed out that in only two months in 2011 (January and February) there were thirteen rebellions by coalition MPs, but mostly by Conservatives. They were over issues such as Europe and fixed-term parliaments (both Conservatives only), postal services (a mix of Liberal Democrats and Conservatives) and the education maintenance allowance (Liberal Democrats only). The Centre also highlighted the fact that backbench Liberal Democrat MPs were rebelling more frequently. While the whole of the previous parliament saw 98 dissenting votes by Liberal Democrats, in its first ten months the coalition suffered 144. However, the Centre points out that while these rebellions show a degree of disagreement and discontent among backbenchers, they are not too worrying for the government because Conservatives and Liberal Democrats have a tendency to rebel over different issues: Conservatives over constitutional affairs such as Europe, and Liberal Democrats over social issues.

Reform of the House of Commons

The public outcry over MPs' expenses was seen as the most forceful expression of a deeper frustration with the political system. Many people began to feel that the House of Commons was not working on their behalf. Therefore, David Cameron's government went on a drive for change. It committed itself to 'recall' elections for those MPs who break parliamentary rules under the Commons Committee on Standards and Privileges.

The government also wants to cut the number of MPs from 650 to 600 and create fewer, more equal-sized constituencies – so that everyone's vote counts, they claim. However, others argue that reducing the number of MPs would only reduce the number of backbench and opposition MPs available to scrutinise legislation and hold the government to account.

They also want to change the present system to a five-year fixed term system and thereby end the personal power of prime ministers to call elections at a time to suit party-political interests. However, to dissolve parliament after a vote of no confidence a 55 per cent majority will be required. This will diminish the power of backbenchers, who previously needed only a simple majority.

The House of Lords

The House of Lords plays an integral role in the legislative process, debating the principles and scrutinising the details of new laws, helping to ensure that legislation is well drafted and effective.

The House of Lords is the second chamber of the UK Parliament and complements the work of the House of Commons. It makes laws, holds the government to account and investigates policy issues with a membership that is mostly appointed. The people who sit in the House of Lords, unlike members of the House of Commons, are not elected and not paid. There are currently around 780 members, known as lords or peers. There are three different types of member: life peers, hereditary peers (who have inherited their title through their family) and bishops. The majority of lords are life peers, chosen because of the work they have done outside parliament. This can include people such as athletes, actors, scientists, doctors, politicians, lawyers and writers.

Table 2.2 **Composition of the House of Lords by party, 1 February 2011**

Party	Life peers	Excepted hereditary peers	Bishops	Total
Conservative	169	48		217
Labour	239	3		242
Liberal Democrats	86	5		91
Crossbench	152	32		184
Bishops			24	24
Other	26	2		28
Total	**672**	**90**	**24**	**786**

This excludes twenty members who are on leave of absence, three who are suspended, fifteen disqualified as senior members of the judiciary and one disqualified as an MEP

Source: www.parliament.uk

Table 2.3 **Composition of the House of Lords by type of peerage, 1 February 2011**

Type	Men	Women	Total
Archbishops and bishops	24	0	24
Life peers under the Appellate Jurisdiction Act (1876)	22	1	23
Life peers under the Life Peerages Act (1958)	510	177	687
Peers under the House of Lords Act (1999)	89	2	91
Total	645	180	825

Source: www.parliament.uk

Lords can also belong to a political party, and some are chosen by the government to work and represent one of their departments. Some lords prefer to be independent and are known as crossbenchers. The expertise of its members and flexibility to scrutinise an issue in depth means that the Lords makes a significant contribution to parliament's work. The House of Lords also has question time, at which questions are answered by a peer. (Each government department has a link peer.)

Making laws

All bills have to pass through both the Commons and the Lords prior to becoming Acts of Parliament. Bills (or draft laws) are debated and scrutinised in both houses.

Legislation takes up about 60 per cent of the House of Lords' time, and members are involved throughout the process of proposing, revising and amending legislation. Some bills introduced by the government begin in the Lords to spread the workload between the two houses; however, the most important bills start in the House of Commons. The House of Lords is well known for the intensity of its scrutiny, often taking an exhaustive line-by-line approach to the detail of a bill, working to highlight potential problems to try to make better and more effective law. It can amend bills and return them to the Commons for consideration and debate. Very often pressure

groups use this stage of the legislative process to try to alter bills, especially if they have difficulty in getting access to Public Bills Committees. While any amendments the Lords make may be disregarded by the House of Commons, it does delay the legislative process and forces the government and House of Commons to rethink the bill and perhaps come up with alternative amendments.

Figure 2.8 **The House of Lords** ↑

In 2011 the House of Lords expressed concern about the wording of the Equality Bill, which allows religious organisations to discriminate on certain grounds when making key religious appointments, and made amendments to it. They also introduced a new clause that allowed civil partnership ceremonies to take place in the premises of religious organisations. All of these amendments were accepted by the House of Commons.

In the last parliament (2005–10), 175 government bills were defeated in the Lords. In the first nine months of Cameron's coalition, twelve bills were defeated, the twelfth being in February 2011 on an amendment to the Parliamentary Voting System and Constituencies Bill to make the result of the referendum on the voting system non-binding if less than 40 per cent of the electorate voted in it.

After much resistance and delays, the Lords voted by 221 to 153 to end their insistence on an amendment that there needed to be a turnout of over 40 per cent. Up to this point the Lords came close to destabilising the coalition, until Liberal Democrats demanded that the prime minister pull his rebel peers into line. They had been supporting Labour and voting in support of the 40 per cent threshold.

In the end Tory rebel peers conceded they had no right to keep forcing the elected Commons to accept their amendment, especially because MPs had voted with a majority in the House of Commons to reject it. The Conservative leader of the Lords, Lord Strathclyde, told peers 'the time has come to respect the will of the elected chamber. We have done our duty.'

Checking the work of the government

Lords check the work of the government by questioning and debating decisions made by ministers and government departments. About 40 per cent of their time is spent on scrutiny.

The House of Lords plays a vital role in scrutinising the work of the government and holding it to account for its decisions and activities. With government ministers sitting in the house and many former ministers and senior politicians and officials among its membership, the House of Lords is well placed to question the government with rigour and insight. Because its members do not represent constituencies and therefore do not need to satisfy the wishes of voters, and are not subject to pressure from whips, they can speak and vote freely on issues. They can also debate controversial issues that are avoided by the House of Commons like abortion and genetic engineering – topics about which MPs are often afraid of exposing their personal opinions in case they upset their constituents and parties.

On a daily basis, peers keep a close eye on the government by asking oral and written questions, responding to government statements or debating key issues. In all cases, the government's reply is a matter of public record, meaning that the House of Lords is able to make a significant contribution to improving transparency and

Fact File

House of Lords key facts, 2009–10

Bills and amendments in the Lords:

- bills handled: 43
- bills receiving royal assent: 30
- amendments tabled: 2,031
- amendments passed: 565.

Lords time spent on legislation and scrutiny, 2010:

- legislation: 55 per cent
  - bills: 47 per cent
  - statutory instruments: 8 per cent.
- scrutiny: 41 per cent
  - debates: 30 per cent
  - questions: 8 per cent
  - statements: 3 per cent
- other: 4 per cent.

Source: www.parliament.uk

the public's understanding of the government's actions.

Questions

Members can ask oral questions on any aspect of the government's activities in the chamber; these are answered by a government minister. While most questions are published in advance, the house has a separate procedure for tabling urgent 'private notice' questions.

There is also the opportunity for written questions; these are used more often, and are used increasingly by members to extract information from the government.

Fact File

House of Lords key facts, 2009–10

Questions:

- oral questions: 248
- written questions: 2906
- statements: 23.

Statements

The government often makes important announcements by means of an oral or written statement to one or both houses of parliament. Following an oral statement to the House of Lords, members are able to question the government minister to raise concerns or seek clarification on any point of policy or fact.

Debates

Debates account for 30 per cent of business in the House of Lords chamber, with members not restricted to debating the legislative programme. They can propose debates on any topic, at the end of which a government minister responds to the questions, concerns and other matters that have been raised.

The professional expertise and specialist knowledge of members are valuable and help to ensure that issues and questions that otherwise might not be highlighted are brought to the government's attention. Because of this, debates in the House of Lords are effective in influencing the decision-making process and help to shape policy and laws.

Throughout 2009–10, during several debates focusing on the economic downturn, peers debated ways to stimulate economic recovery and growth in the UK. Professional expertise and specialist knowledge were provided by members who were business leaders and senior economists, each contributing the benefits of their first-hand experience. There were also three debates on education, about the contribution of modern languages to the UK economy, teaching excellence, and cuts to funding for higher and further education. Again, professional expertise and specialist knowledge were provided by members who were former teachers and principals of various universities throughout the UK.

Fact File

House of Lords key facts, 2009–10

Debates:

- general debates: 39
- short debates: 18
- debates on committee reports: 15.

Specialist committees

Committee work takes place outside the chamber. There are permanent committees investigating work relating to Europe, science and technology, economics, communications and the constitution. Occasionally, one-off committees are set up to deal with issues outside these areas.

Committees in the House of Lords have a different function to those in the Commons. Each Lords committee focuses on a broad subject area rather than a particular government department. They also benefit from the specialist knowledge and wide range of experience of their members. This allows for a more rigorous and independent approach to scrutiny.

Fact File

House of Lords committees

Communications Committee

The Communications Committee looks at issues regarding the media and creative industries.

Constitution Committee

The Constitution Committee scrutinises public bills raising significant constitutional issues, considers broader government policy affecting the constitution, and keeps the operation of the UK constitution under review.

Economic Affairs Committee

The Economic Affairs Committee holds inquiries into specific economic issues and scrutinises aspects of the Finance Bill.

European Union Committee

The European Union Committee conducts inquiries into and scrutinises in detail European Commission proposals for new policies and regulations.

Science and Technology Committee

The Science and Technology Committee covers a wide range of science policy matters, many of which have a significant impact on UK national policy decisions.

Fact File

Policy impact post-1999

As a result of changes in party balance, and because of a constant influx of new members, the mood in the House of Lords changed after 1999 – it became more assertive. Peers began to consider themselves more entitled to challenge government policy. When the Liberal Democrats voted with the Conservatives in the Lords, the two parties could defeat the Labour governments of 1997–2010. (The votes of independent crossbenchers rarely affected the outcome because they tended to split.) From 1997 to 2010, the Labour government suffered 514 defeats in the House of Lords. In comparison, there were just six government defeats during this time in the House of Commons.

Research shows that although in theory the Commons could overturn all Lords defeats, the government gives in to the Lords about half of the time. Hence there were around 200 occasions when a Lords defeat resulted in a change to Labour government policy between 1997 and 2010.

Activities

1. Explain what the role of the monarchy is in parliament.

2. Explain what is meant by prerogative powers.

3. Describe the key functions of the House of Commons.

4. What are the two most important stages in the passage of a bill in the House of Commons? Why is this?

5. What is the difference between a private members' bill and a government bill, and which has the better chance of success?

6. Explain in detail the ways in which backbench MPs can scrutinise the government.

7. To what extent can select committees effectively scrutinise the government's actions?

8. MPs truly reflect today's society. Discuss.

9. Explain what the role of the House of Lords is in parliament.

10. Describe the key functions of the House of Lords.

Essay question

Backbench MPs have little influence on decision making in central government. Discuss.

The Executive

The UK Executive is made up of three parts as follows:

- the prime minister
- the cabinet
- the civil service.

The Executive is mainly involved in formulating and implementing government policy. The prime minister and the cabinet are politically motivated and partisan in their decision-making capacity, whereas the civil service is politically neutral with a predominantly administrative function.

The role of the prime minister

The draft cabinet manual of December 2010 summarises the role of the prime minister as follows:

> The Prime Minister is the head of government by virtue of his or her ability to command the confidence of the House of Commons. He or she is appointed by the Sovereign and in turn recommends to the Sovereign the appointment of ministers to the Government … The Prime Minister is also responsible for the organisation of government and the allocation of functions between ministers, who derive their powers from statute, the Royal Prerogative and the common law. The Prime Minister, advised by the Cabinet Secretary, may make changes to the machinery of government.
>
> (Coalition Agreement 2010)

The prime minister is chosen by the monarch, who through constitutional convention picks the person who has the support of the House of Commons; this is usually the leader of the largest political party in the Commons. In fact, as the head of government, the prime minister is ultimately responsible for the policy and decisions of the government. He or she also oversees the operation of the civil service and government agencies, appoints members of the cabinet and is the principal government figure in the House of Commons. For this reason it is important that the prime minister controls the House of Commons and does not lose their confidence in him or her. If this happens the Commons can pass a vote of no confidence, leading to the resignation of the prime minister and the government. This happened to the minority Labour Government of James Callaghan in 1979. In the election that followed, the Conservatives, under Margaret Thatcher, came to power. Labour did not form a government again until 1997, when Tony Blair won with a landslide victory.

Powers of the prime minister

The sources of the prime minister's powers give him or her the authority to exert them; this authority can be transient, and therefore varies between each prime minister.

Figure 2.9 David Cameron ←

Five sources of prime ministerial power

The monarch
The prime minister holds prerogative powers that afford him or her traditional authority.

The party
The prime minister is the majority party leader; this confers power and authority as head of government that is both legal and rational.

The people
It could be argued that although the prime minister is not directly elected by the people, most people vote for a leader as well as a party; therefore, indirectly he or she has the people's authority. This could be called charismatic authority.

Parliament
As long as he or she has a majority in and the confidence of the House of Commons, the prime minister has the authority of parliament.

The cabinet
As cabinet chairperson, the prime minister has the authority of the cabinet.

Power of appointment/dismissal
The power to appoint and dismiss government ministers – especially cabinet ministers – is arguably where most of the prime minister's power lies. It is the prime minister who decides which MPs to reward or punish by appointing them to specific posts and including or excluding them from the cabinet. This power to 'hire' or 'fire' includes the power to 'reshuffle' (or refresh) the make-up of the cabinet or government whenever he or she deems it necessary. This can allow the prime minister to create a cabinet of loyal supporters; however, in reality it is best to consider the selection carefully, paying close attention to people's ambitions. If someone is overlooked for promotion they can become resentful, and it is important for the prime minister to retain the support and loyalty of all his or her MPs. In his memoirs Tony Blair calls those left out as the 'ejected, dejected and rejected' who eventually come to 'resent you'.

In his cabinet reshuffle of 2006, Blair ejected Charles Clarke from the post of Home Secretary. Clarke was so annoyed and dejected that he refused the post of Defence Secretary and instead returned to the back benches. Similarly Jack Straw was ejected as Foreign Secretary, and Blair said Straw was 'upset at being replaced'. On the other hand, Blair was forced to include Gordon Brown in the cabinet as Chancellor of the Exchequer from 1997 until his own resignation in 2007, and was effectively powerless to remove him. In his memoirs Blair wrote that this reshuffle saw him make 'a sort of "worst of all worlds" set of decisions … all in all, a mess at the wrong time and with the wrong people, who I needed onside'.

When Gordon Brown took over as prime minister in 2007 he swiftly made changes to the cabinet in a conscious effort to give the message that he was in charge and it was now a Brown cabinet not a continuing Blair one. He also rewarded his own loyal supporters like Ed Balls – his 'right-hand man' at the Treasury for the previous ten years – who became Secretary of State for Education. In fact he only retained one minister in post, Des Browne as Defence Secretary, but he combined that post with the Scotland Office and reduced the number in the cabinet from 23 to 22. Brown subsequently reshuffled his cabinet in 2009. He rejected Margaret Beckett for promotion, who subsequently resigned from the front bench. Like Blair, he also had trouble ejecting his chancellor – Alistair Darling – who it was rumoured refused to move to the Home Office and so kept his job as Chancellor of the Exchequer.

Figure 2.10 Tony Blair and Gordon Brown ↑

Similarly, as part of the coalition agreement in 2010, David Cameron could only allocate cabinet posts after consulting Nick Clegg, and any subsequent allocations had to be agreed between the prime minister and the deputy prime minister. However, after only nine months as

prime minister Cameron faced pressure from his own Tory MPs to reshuffle his cabinet following concerns that the government was failing to get its message across.

Composition of the Government

1.1 The initial allocation of cabinet, Ministerial, Whip and Special Adviser appointments between the two Parties was agreed between the Prime Minister and the Deputy Prime Minister.

1.2 Future allocation will continue to be based on the principle that the Parliamentary Party with fewer MPs will have a share of cabinet, Ministerial and Whip appointments agreed between the Prime Minister and the Deputy Prime Minister, approximately in proportion to the size of the two Parliamentary Parties. The Prime Minister and the Deputy Prime Minister will agree the nomination of the Law Officers.

1.3 Any changes to the allocation of portfolios between the Parliamentary Parties during the lifetime of the Coalition will be agreed between the Prime Minister and the Deputy Prime Minister.

1.4 No Liberal Democrat Minister or Whip may be removed on the recommendation of the Prime Minister without full consultation with the Deputy Prime Minister.

(Coalition Agreement 2010)

Power of patronage

The prime minister also has the power to be involved in appointing people to important positions outside the government. For example, he or she can make political nominations to the House of Lords and is allowed to approve one person for a top ecclesiastical appointment in the Church of England. In 2010 Dolar Popat

– a Ugandan-born, Indian former refugee and self-made multi-millionaire who has given the Tories more than £200,000 in donations – was given a seat in the House of Lords by Cameron. Also, film director and screenwriter Julian Fellowes, the creator of hit ITV period drama *Downton Abbey*, was made a Conservative peer along with former BBC chairman Michael Grade, former BMI owner Sir Michael Bishop and divorce lawyer Fiona Shackleton, whose clients have included Sir Paul McCartney and the Prince of Wales.

Majority party leadership

As the leader of the largest party in the House of Commons, the prime minister usually has a majority and therefore a position of confidence to successfully carry out his or her government's programme. Having been elected by the party it is generally possible to maintain strong party discipline with the help of the whip system; this, coupled with the power to set the parliamentary timetable, gives him or her the power to control the legislative process.

Blair commanded great power and authority in his first two terms in office but this ebbed away until 2007, when he left office earlier than intended. David Cameron had to form a coalition to establish a Commons majority but lost the support of some MPs because of the compromises he made.

Power of dissolution

The prime minister can use the prerogative power to dissolve parliament and hold a general election. Margaret Thatcher and Tony Blair used this power wisely. In 2001 and 2005, Tony Blair called an election with one year of the five-year parliament still to run.

The power of dissolution can also be a double-edged sword, as experienced by Gordon Brown shortly after he became prime minister following Tony Blair's resignation. Opinion polls in early autumn gave Labour a lead over the Conservatives and Brown's advisers implied that the prime minister was considering holding a snap election. However, the Conservatives' October party conference reduced the gap between the two parties and no election was held. Brown was accused of losing his nerve and being indecisive. The Liberal Democrat MP Vince Cable stated that Brown appeared to have been transformed 'from Stalin to Mr Bean'.

Figure 2.11 Gordon Brown: 'from Stalin to Mr Bean'?

Cabinet chairperson

The prime minister chairs cabinet meetings, and in so doing has the power to set the agenda and determine what is discussed and – in some cases more importantly – what is not discussed. He or she also controls the pace and direction of the meetings and sums up the 'sense' of what took place. This allows the prime minister to have a dominant role in cabinet.

Image and popularity

Prime ministers rely on the support of the people, and need to remain popular and appear statesmanlike. They attract much media attention and live with a high degree of public scrutiny as spokesperson for the government. They also provide national leadership at home and on the international stage, leading the nation in times of crisis and emergency. They sit down with other world leaders and attend high-profile meetings with the world's government leaders such as at the G8 and EU summits. They are directly involved in foreign policy, and it is the prime minister who negotiates treaties. A popular and well-liked prime minister will have the support of the people and this will be reflected in high ratings in the polls. This in turn gives him or her the authority to act on behalf of the people and maintain flexibility in matters of policy, more so than a disliked or weak prime minister.

Blair received high poll ratings throughout his first term in office but this slipped after the weapons of mass destruction (WMD) episode and the subsequent war in Iraq, when he lost the trust of many people. Brown came to office with a strong reputation for economic competence after ten years as chancellor; however, the worldwide recession and global credit crunch undermined his credibility as prime minister. In addition, his perceived lack of charisma and personality resulted in his ratings plummeting throughout 2009 and up to the election in 2010.

Policy maker
The prime minister's policy-making role is broad and is not confined to one department like other ministers.

Limits on the power of the prime minister

Powerful colleagues
In theory, the prime minister has the ability to create a cabinet in his or her own image. In reality, a prime minister's power within the cabinet is limited by a need to assuage the ambitions of party colleagues. Senior party members and those who have been loyal and show potential may expect to be included in the government regardless of their own personal political views. The prime minister is also restricted by the pool of MPs that is available; while it is his or her only resource, it can also

provide obstacles. Subsequently, the prime minister may be pushed into offering positions to potential rivals and opponents: these people may be less trouble inside the cabinet, where they are bound by the convention of collective responsibility, rather than outside it on the back benches – where they could stir up dissent and be a focus for rebels should a policy be controversial.

Margaret Thatcher, Conservative prime minister from 1979 to 1990, was regarded as a strong and effective leader. Yet 'the Iron Lady' was effectively forced out of office by her cabinet colleagues in November 1990, thus demonstrating the limitation of the office of the prime minister.

Figure 2.12 Margaret Thatcher leaving 10 Downing Street in 1990

Prime Minister Cameron had trouble with the right of his party in his first year in office. This was because of his policies on giving prisoners the vote, his Home Secretary's liberal views on law and order, and the cuts to the defence budget while the international aid budget was maintained. In fact, Cameron saw more of his own MPs rebel and faced more revolts in his first year in office than Tony Blair during the whole of his first term.

Cameron brought the former Conservative leader William Hague into the cabinet as Foreign Secretary in 2010 to shore up his own position, and then was reluctant to oust him when things started to go wrong. Mr Hague faced criticism over his handling of the crisis in Libya in 2011. He came under fire for a botched SAS and MI6 mission to contact rebel groups in eastern Libya and for mistakenly suggesting that the Libyan dictator Gaddafi had fled the country for Venezuela. It was suggested at the time that criticism of Hague in the media was being fuelled privately by other cabinet ministers, who claimed he had lost his 'mojo' and should step down. These differences of opinion on foreign policy caused friction within the cabinet.

Party support

It is important that the prime minister retains the support of the party through good and bad times. It is the party members who elect the leader; without their support, the prime minister would not be leader and therefore could not be the premier. Tony Blair was never challenged as party leader and Gordon Brown was elected unopposed to take over as party leader. When David Cameron was elected leader of the Conservatives with almost 70 per cent of party members' votes, he said he would use the broad 'mandate' that the party had given him to expand his authority. He voiced his belief that as leader he was the most important member of the cabinet.

As some Conservative MPs begin to show a restlessness and frustration at having to share power with the Liberal Democrats while waiting for that promotion that might never come, it is worth noting that three of Cameron's six predecessors were forced out by leadership elections.

Public opinion

The prime minister can be limited in achieving his or her aims through a lack of support from the general public. Changing the UK voting system was taken out of the hands of the government and placed into the hands of the people through a referendum.

Events

Several key events limited Gordon Brown's power as prime minister and eventually led to his defeat at the polls in 2010. For example, the global financial crisis, the unexpected backlash over the Gurkha resettlement issue, the damaging MPs' expenses controversies and the 'bigotgate' incident (see pages 30–31), followed by the resignations of several key cabinet members, were just some of the events during his premiership that indicated his dwindling power and support. Moreover, while his performance in the leaders' debates improved and he grew in confidence with each subsequent contest, in the eyes of the electorate he failed to make enough of an impression.

The opposition

The 'official opposition' is the largest minority party, and its main purpose is to oppose the government of the day. However, the leader of the opposition occasionally has to decide whether to set aside that purpose and offer limited cooperation to the prime minister – for instance, when the prime minister offers access to confidential official information or an invitation to enter into consultations on government policy. He or she must also be prepared, in the event of the resignation of the government, to assume office as prime minister.

There is a leader of the opposition in both the House of Commons and the House of Lords. As leader of the largest opposition party (Labour), Ed Miliband is the current leader of the opposition in the Commons. The leader of the opposition picks a 'shadow cabinet' to follow and scrutinise the work of each government department and the policies being developed in their specific areas.

Former Labour cabinet and shadow cabinet member Tessa Jowell said that 'the good opposition challenges government decisions in a ruthless, disciplined way but also campaigns in a way that allows fires of protest to be lit.'

Prime ministerial style

Gordon Brown's style was that of a hands-on leader, involved in the detail and the doing of the work rather than delegating – especially when it came to special aides. He was seen as having less of a 'sofa'-style government than Blair, but still gave only a limited role to the cabinet. He came across to most people as a committed prime minister, but austere and with poor communication and people skills.

According to Alastair Campbell, there are two somewhat conflicting aspects of David Cameron's style of leadership. On the one hand he has taken to the job of prime minister as to the manor born: his time at Eton has given him an inner and outer confidence that he puts to good use. On the other hand when it comes to policy detail, Campbell feels he does not go deep enough and so risks appearing to be making it up as he goes along.

The cabinet

The cabinet is at the heart of the British political system and is the supreme decision-making body in government, being typically made up of around 20 to 25 members. It is essentially a government committee that is chaired by the prime minister and whose members are ministers in charge of departments. The prime minister has traditionally been referred to as *primus inter pares*, which means 'first among equals', and demonstrates that he or she is a member of the collective decision-making body of the cabinet, rather than an individual who has powers in their own right. The prime minister is first among equals simply in recognition of the responsibility held for appointing and dismissing all the other cabinet members. This can make ministers feel that they are beholden to the prime minister and owe him or her their loyalty. However, the prime minister relies on the support of the cabinet and so must be careful not

to alienate any ministers. As part of the cabinet, it is important to support its collective decisions. It is a case of 'united we stand, divided we fall': a divided cabinet is a serious bleeding of prime ministerial power. Gordon Brown faced a divided cabinet over his leadership of the party in the run-up to the 2010 election, and this significantly diluted his power as prime minister. Divisions were already evident over whether Labour should have pursued a 'class war' campaign against David Cameron in 2009, and an attempted coup four months before the election even had the backing of some cabinet ministers. The table in the cabinet room is deliberately oval-shaped so that the prime minister, who sits in the centre of one of the long sides, can see the faces and body language of all the cabinet and so spot any little signs of loyalty or dissent.

Cabinet ministers are the most senior ministers in the government and are also known as secretaries of state, with each heading a government department. Every Tuesday during parliament, secretaries of state from all departments and some other ministers meet in the cabinet room in Downing Street to discuss the most important issues of the day. The cabinet is a demonstration of the collective strength of government and is bound by the convention of collective responsibility. The prime minister

Figure 2.13 The cabinet usually has between 20 and 25 members ↑

chairs the meeting and sets its agenda; he also decides who speaks around the cabinet table and sums up at the end of each item. It is this summing up that becomes government policy, with all members being collectively responsible for all decisions and policies. The secretary of the cabinet is responsible for preparing records of its discussions and decisions.

Powers of cabinet

The cabinet has no legal powers; any powers that are assumed to lie with the cabinet are actually held by secretaries of state. It does have a collective responsibility to parliament, so all members are bound to support cabinet decisions even if they were not present when they were made. Its main function is to legislate and agree the presentation of government policy. It also arranges the daily business of parliament on behalf of the government and is the final arbiter of disputes involving ministers that must be kept within the cabinet.

As the complexity of government decision making has evolved, more agents have become involved. Prime ministers are now more likely to consult with external think tanks, cabinet committees and special advisers before making decisions. For example, the Cabinet Office Briefing Room A (COBRA), which has both ministers and non-government officials, takes decisions on national security in emergency situations. This leads to the perception that the cabinet may be less important than it once was, and is only there to rubber-stamp decisions that have already been made or to present government policy and decisions.

The Cabinet Office

The Cabinet Office lies at the very centre of government, with an overarching purpose of making government work better. It supports the prime minister and the cabinet, helping to ensure effective development, co-ordination and implementation of policy and operations across all government departments.

Cabinet committees

Much of the work of cabinet is delegated to committees. These committees can reduce the burden on cabinet by enabling collective decisions to be made by a smaller group of ministers who are able to deal more efficiently with the large volume of government business. Often, the need for quick decision making means that it is not possible to involve the whole cabinet in many policy decisions. Consequently, the prime minister selects a smaller group of around four or five ministers to form committees; they can come up with policies and present them to the prime minister and cabinet more quickly.

Some of the committees are permanent while others are only set up for a short period of time to deal with particular issues. Cabinet committees now handle the majority of cabinet work, and the decisions they make have the authority of the full cabinet. In the event that a committee cannot agree and come to a decision on an issue, it will be sent to the full cabinet for a final decision.

The composition and terms of reference of coalition cabinet committees are a matter for the prime minister, in consultation with the deputy prime minister. Each committee has a chair from one party and a deputy chair from the other. David Cameron is limited in his choice of members because he must fully consult Nick Clegg on everything from policy to cabinet positions. If he wishes to remove a Liberal Democrat MP from the cabinet, he has to agree it with Clegg first. Under Tony Blair the cabinet met infrequently, but under Cameron cabinet government has risen in importance because of the need for collegiality and consultation to make the coalition work. However, this arrangement put the convention of collective responsibility under strain as government members were forced to support policies in public that they had opposed in their manifestos. For example, Nick Clegg later admitted that he 'should have been more careful' about signing the pre-election pledge to oppose any increase in tuition fees.

Collective responsibility

Collective responsibility is at the heart of cabinet government. The cabinet tries to reach decisions on the basis that as members of the government, ministers are collectively responsible and have to publicly support and defend those decisions regardless of their personal opinions – or resign. For example, both Robin Cook and Clare Short resigned from the Labour government in 2003 over the war in Iraq; meanwhile, in 2009 communities secretary Hazel Blears resigned after publicly criticising the government's performance, as did work and pensions secretary James Purnell, who felt he could no longer publicly support Gordon Brown and called for the prime minister to stand aside.

Coalition agreement for stability and reform

The Ministerial Code is the Prime Minister's guidance to his Ministers on how he expects them to undertake their official duties.

The principle of collective responsibility still applies to all Government Ministers within the Coalition and requires:

● an appropriate degree of consultation and discussion among Ministers to provide the opportunity for them to express their views frankly as decisions are reached, and to ensure the support of all Ministers

● the opinions expressed and advice offered within Government to remain private

● decisions of the Cabinet to be binding on and supported by all Ministers.

(Coalition Agreement 2010)

Individual ministerial responsibility

Individual ministerial responsibility ensures that ministers are accountable to parliament and the public for their own personal conduct and that of the department they run. This doctrine implies that ministers are ultimately accountable and should take full responsibility for their own or their department's mistakes and resign. This is even expected of them should the mistake not be their own but that of civil servants in the department in order to maintain the anonymity of civil servants.

For example, in 2010 David Laws made history when he became the shortest-serving cabinet member in modern British political history. The Liberal Democrat MP served as chief secretary to the Treasury for just sixteen days before it was discovered that he had claimed expenses that he should not have claimed and resigned. He said 'the public is entitled to expect politicians to act with a sense of responsibility for our actions ... I do not see how I can carry out my crucial work on the Budget and spending review while I have to deal with the private and public implications of recent revelations.'

However, in reality ministers rarely resign over the fault of others, under the claim that they must not be held to account for the actions and mistakes of others over which they had no control. For example, controversy raged in

Figure 2.14 Vince Cable ←

2011 when business secretary Vince Cable did not resign and was not sacked from the cabinet despite 'declaring war' on Rupert Murdoch, and David Cameron saying that his comments about Murdoch were 'totally unacceptable and inappropriate'.

In response, the Labour leader Ed Miliband said he would have sacked Mr Cable:

'Having apparently breached the ministerial code and having said what he said, he shouldn't be remaining in office and I fear that David Cameron has made this decision not because it's good for the country, but because he is worried about the impact on his coalition of Vince Cable going. That's not the way decisions about who is in and out of government should be made.'

The civil service

The civil service is led by the cabinet secretary. The most senior civil servant in a department is a permanent secretary. Each supports the government minister who heads their department and is accountable to parliament for the department's actions and performance. The permanent secretary is the 'accounting officer' for their department, reporting to parliament. They must make sure their department spends the money allocated to them appropriately. The permanent secretary leading a department is also responsible to the cabinet secretary and head of the home civil service for the effective day-to-day management of their department and its civil servants. Each department handles an aspect of government policy: for example, home affairs or education. They are responsible for policy making in their sector, and in many cases for the service delivery as well. There are currently nineteen ministerial departments and twenty non-ministerial departments.

The civil service helps the government of the day to develop and deliver its policies as effectively as possible. They are career-minded

Figure 2.15 The Home Office ↑

permanent employees of the government, and unlike MPs they are appointed not elected and must be politically neutral. The role of the senior civil service is to offer impartial advice to ministers and inform them of the possible consequences and the potential advantages and disadvantages of their actions or decisions. There are around 500,000 civil servants in the UK, with about 4000 senior civil servants and around 200 most senior officials. They are permanent in the sense that their appointment means they cannot be removed by a dissatisfied minister or at election time. This continuity of tenure allows them to build up experience and expertise that is usually lacking in a minister, and enables them to offer genuinely neutral advice without the worry of any personal political implications. It also means that, because of the high turnover of government ministers, they are likely to serve many ministers. It has been calculated that the average tenure of a government minister in the Brown government was just 1.3 years, with junior ministers being moved more or less on an annual basis.

Special advisers

A special adviser or 'spad' is a minister's principal political confidant, advising, liaising and most famously spinning the party view. When you read in a newspaper comments by an 'aide' to a minister or 'sources close to the minister', that's usually the spad commenting.

Spads hold a privileged and special role in government. Like civil servants, they are paid by the taxpayer but they do not need to be politically neutral. Whereas civil servants offer neutral advice to ministers, spads offer political advice. Their key purpose has been described as 'devilling', or 'squirrelling' away at all government policy and communications to ensure that it complies with or 'toes' the appropriate party or political line. Whereas civil servants must not engage in any political activity that could be interpreted as compromising their independence and must promise to act impartially, spads are openly political but cannot override advice from officials that they find unpalatable.

With the exception of the prime minister and his or her deputy, cabinet ministers generally have just two spads each. Prime Minister David Cameron approved the appointment of every special adviser. In his biography, Tony Blair admits to having accumulated 70 at one point – 'considered by some to be a bit of a constitutional outrage', he adds. However, he saw them as essential to speeding up the process of political decision making and a sensible way of enlarging the scope of available advice.

Unlike the appointment of civil servants, there is no merit-based process to that of the spad. Ministers simply choose whoever they reckon is best for the job; the only restriction is that the prime minister must approve every appointment.

In 2011, David Cameron was officially reprimanded by the head of the civil service over what was called the 'unacceptable' behaviour of some of his special advisers. The cabinet secretary, Sir Gus O'Donnell, wrote a strongly worded letter to the prime minister urging him to restrain government aides accused of 'smearing' the head of the Electoral Commission. He was said to have been furious after reading a newspaper report describing a former Audit Commission board member as 'incompetent'.

The incident only came to light after a response to a Freedom of Information request confirmed that Sir Gus had written to the prime minister to discuss 'the role, status or conduct of government special advisers'. A source close to a minister spoke of mounting concern in Whitehall about the activities of some Tory special advisers, saying that the devilish behaviour was the final straw for Sir Gus, who wrote in his letter to Cameron 'this is unacceptable behaviour' and 'please rein in your spads'.

This incident highlights the controversial role of spads and the conflicts that can arise between official civil servants and 'temporary civil servants' or special advisers. Further scrutiny of the Executive followed this incident, with calls from Labour for David Cameron to come clean about whether or not advisers were responsible for what they called 'these disgraceful negative briefings'. Labour demanded that if they were, then they should be sacked; since coming to power, the Conservatives had warned all their new special advisers that if they leaked information to the press they would be fired.

Gordon Brown's special adviser and press spokesman Damian McBride was forced to resign in 2009 after he was exposed plotting to smear senior Tories. This followed on from the most public dispute between senior civil servants and spin doctors which occurred in 2002 (see page 64, 'Politicisation of the civil service').

Politicisation of the civil service

In September 2001 Jo Moore, the spin doctor of Stephen Byers, minister for the Department of Transport, Local Government and the Regions (DTLR), had faced calls for her resignation when it became known that she had advised 'burying bad news' by issuing departmental press releases immediately after the 9/11 terrorist attacks.

Byers protected her, but Moore was forced to offer a public apology for her behaviour.

Relations between Moore and the senior civil servants within the department, including the director of communications, Martin Sixsmith, were strained and hostile. In February 2002, more allegations against Jo Moore were leaked and she agreed to resign after Byers promised that Sixsmith would also be forced to resign. Byers informed the House of Commons that he had accepted Sixsmith's resignation. This was untrue because Sixsmith had not offered his resignation. Byers was forced to resign because he had told the house a direct lie.

As the *Sunday Times* stated, the whole affair highlighted 'a ministry in chaos and a government staffed by *apparatchiks* who had lost contact with the truth'.

Figure 2.16 Martin Sixsmith ↑

Table 2.4 **The roles of ministers, senior civil servants and special advisers**

Ministers	Senior civil servants	Special advisers
Elected MPs	Appointed by the Crown	Appointed by ministers
Formulate government policy	Impartial advice on policy	Partial advice on policy
Collectively responsible for government policy	Politically neutral	Politically motivated
Accountable to parliament	Anonymous	Accountable to ministers
Temporary	Permanent	Temporary

Activities

1 Describe what the Executive is.

2 Explain the role of the prime minister.

3 What are the sources of the prime minister's power?

4 Explain the main powers of the prime minister.

5 Explain the main limits on the powers of the prime minister.

6 What is the role of the cabinet?

7 Describe the powers of the cabinet.

8 What is the role of cabinet committees?

9 What is meant by collective responsibility?

10 What is meant by individual ministerial responsibility?

11 Explain the difference between the civil service and special advisers.

Essay question

To what extent can parliament control the powers of the prime minister?

Pressure groups

Twenty-first-century politics in the UK is characterised by attempts to involve more people and increase participation in the decision-making process. Prime Minister Cameron spoke of a society where more and more people are involved in the legislative process. No longer should participation be restricted to voting and joining a political party, he said.

Political parties do provide a necessary link between ordinary citizens and government. However, for some the diverse range of policies and issues they address is too broad. Pressure groups offer a narrower and more specific focus, usually on a single issue that can seem more important and more appealing to many.

As a result, pressure groups have become more commonplace in the UK as an additional route to the decision makers. This is especially true for young people who do not yet have the vote and those who feel left behind and disillusioned by mainstream representative democracy.

The UK has one of the lowest rates of political party membership in Europe: membership of the Conservative and Labour party is about 200 000 each. On the other hand, Historic Scotland has 103,747 members, the National Trust has around 309,000, Friends of the Earth International has over 2 million members and Greenpeace has 2.9 million. Also, as voter turnout declines membership of pressure groups is on the increase. Table 2.5 shows the decline of voter turnout between 1950 and 2010.

Figure 2.17 Friends of the Earth International has over 2 million members ↑

However, the role and effectiveness of pressure groups in influencing the decision-making process of a democratic system are hotly debated subjects. While some argue that they threaten democracy, others argue that they actually enhance the democratic process. Also, just how influential are pressure groups and why are some more successful than others? This chapter will address these issues.

Table 2.5 Turnout at general elections, 1950–2010 (%, selected years)

Year	UK	Scotland
2010	65.1	63.8
2005	61.4	60.8
2001	59.4	58.2
1997	71.4	71.3
1992	77.7	75.5
1983	72.7	72.7
1979	76	76.8
1974 (Feb)	78.8	79
1966	75.8	76
1959	78.7	78.1
1951	82.6	81.2
1950	83.9	80.9

Source: House of Commons Research Papers

What is a pressure group?

A pressure group is a group of like-minded individuals who want to influence the decision makers. They do not want to be the government, but they do want to put pressure on the government to take into account their views when formulating policy or passing new legislation. They may also want to put pressure on MPs and peers to consider their opinions and have existing laws amended or revoked.

Types of pressure groups

Pressure groups can be classified either by their aims or in terms of the nature of their relationship with the government. Cause and sectional groups are so called because of their core aims; insider and outsider groups are known as such because of the nature of their relationship with the government.

Cause groups

Members of cause groups usually have a shared belief or view, and are set up to promote a particular cause that has nothing to do with its members' material welfare. For this reason they are sometimes known as 'public interest groups': they look after the interests of society as a whole. They can be in existence for a short period or over the longer term. For example, the Friends of the Roseburn Urban Wildlife Corridor were a cause group set up with the aim of preventing the return of trams to Edinburgh's streets. They were a temporary group and they campaigned while this was an issue, but disbanded afterwards. On the other hand, a cause group such as the Child Poverty Action Group, which aims to eradicate child poverty, has been around for a longer period.

Figure 2.18 The Friends of the Roseburn Urban Wildlife Corridor were unsuccessful in their bid to prevent the return of trams to Edinburgh ↑

Sectional groups

Sectional groups are set up to represent and promote the material interests of a specific section of society. For this reason, they are sometimes known as 'private interest groups': they look after the interest of their members. The most popular form of sectional group is a trade union, which looks after the material interests of workers according to their occupation. For example, the Educational Institute of Scotland (EIS) looks after the interests of Scottish teachers and the British Medical Association (BMA) looks after the interests of doctors. This makes them restrictive in their membership, because you have to be a teacher or a doctor to join these groups.

Usually sectional groups have more success in influencing the decision-making process because they are generally better organised and have the power of threatening industrial action by their members. Cause groups do not have this power because their members come from a variety of backgrounds and occupations.

Insider or outsider?

As well as characterising pressure groups as cause or sectional, we can also categorise them according to the nature of their relationship with the government. Those with a close working relationship have insider status and are known as insider groups, while those without such a relationship have outsider status and are known as outsider groups.

Insider pressure groups

Insider pressure groups can be thought of as having a special relationship with the government because their views and objectives are likely to be compatible with those of the government. They tend to have a closer and more personal two-way dialogue with the policy makers at an early stage in policy formulation, and work in an environment of mutual trust and respect. The government recognises them as being well informed and having expert knowledge, and therefore useful. When formulating policy or making decisions on an issue, insider groups would expect to be consulted and have their views listened to. They would normally offer expert advice to the government while respecting the right of the government to make decisions after proper consultation. For example, the BMA has medical experts who can advise the government on

health policy from the inside. The SNP minority government consulted with the BMA prior to its decision to introduce free prescriptions. The BMA supported this proposal, and in April 2011 prescription charges were abolished.

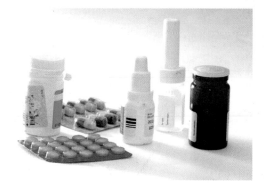

Figure 2.19 Prescription charges have been abolished in Scotland ↑

Outsider pressure groups

As the name suggests, outsider pressure groups tend to have views and objectives that are seen as being incompatible or even seriously out of step with those of the government. Therefore, they lack any close or special relationship with the government and are unlikely to be consulted; they are seen as being left outside the policy-formulation process. They also lack any formal recognition and often attempt to attract the support of the public as a means of legitimisation. For example, Greenpeace reject any formal relationship with government, instead

Figure 2.20 Greenpeace campaigns for a sustainable world ↑

choosing to mobilise public and media support and thereby put pressure on government to achieve their aims from the outside.

Table 2.6 Insider and outsider pressure groups

Insiders	Outsiders
Are compatible with the government	Are incompatible with the government
Are regularly consulted by the decision makers	Are not generally consulted
Work with the government	Engage in direct action and civil disobedience to put pressure on the decision makers
Have privileged status	Not seen as having useful expertise or objectivity
Have expert knowledge	Usually campaign on controversial issues

What role do pressure groups play in the UK?

Today, pressure groups have three main roles or functions:

- representation
- participation
- education.

Representation

Pressure groups provide a means of representation for those who feel their needs are not being met by political parties. Whereas parties try to cater for large and diverse views in society, pressure groups tend to be more focused and concentrate on specific issues. For example, a person may join and support a pressure group campaigning against animal testing while voting for a party that supports it.

They can also help to prevent the 'tyranny of the majority' by providing representation for minority groups whose views may be overlooked; for example, the Terence Higgins Trust provides a voice for those living with HIV.

Participation

Pressure groups allow citizens the opportunity to participate in the political process between elections. They are also a vehicle for those below the voting age to have a voice; indeed, the forms of direct action that are mainly associated with outsider groups tend to attract young people. Pressure groups can also increase participation by helping to devolve decision-making power from what is referred to as the traditional centre.

Education

Pressure groups can educate the general public about the actions and policies of the government. Many groups closely scrutinise and monitor the activities of the government and raise issues in the public domain through the media and other means. They can also stimulate debate on issues – for example, over the trams in Edinburgh – by educating the public and policy makers about both sides of the argument.

Methods used by pressure groups

Some pressure groups with insider status have regular contact with and are consulted by the decision makers, and thereby have the ability to influence policy at an early stage. Others have to be more proactive.

Contacting MPs

Individual members can write, email or telephone MPs directly to express their views on an issue or policy, and can question their own MP's stance. This can be very effective because MPs are up for re-election every five years and are reliant on the votes of their constituents.

Pressure group members can also attempt to influence MPs who are members of select committees or the Public Bill Committee. They could do this themselves, or they could employ a professional lobbyist to make contact with MPs and present the views of the pressure group on their behalf. It has been claimed that professional lobbyists were used to pressurise MPs over the decision to close RAF Kinloss and cancel the contract for the new Nimrod MRA4 aircraft.

Contacting peers

This is especially influential when the House of Lords is debating a bill that has come through the House of Commons. Pressure groups can attempt to court the support of the peers to amend bills and help get them accepted by the Commons.

Direct action

Direct action is a tactic usually employed by outsider pressure groups who feel that other methods of influencing policy have failed and that a more direct approach to attract attention is required. Action that involves protests, marches and in some cases civil disobedience can have the effect of raising public awareness or even just allowing a voice to be heard, and in so doing apply direct pressure on decision makers.

Throughout 2010 and 2011, climate change protesters in Edinburgh resorted to direct action in response to the Royal Bank of Scotland's investment in oil industry developments around the world. This involved throwing an oil-like substance onto a busy dual carriageway and at buildings, and also smashing windows. One protestor commented that 'amongst protesters, there are differences of opinion about what direct action to take. We're really just trying to raise awareness because sometimes it's so hard to get attention on these issues unless some people go out there and really try to draw that attention.'

Figure 2.21 Climate change protesters in Edinburgh ↑

However, violent and illegal direct action drew criticism from some student protestors during the demonstrations against tuition fees in 2010. Violent protestors were seen as the 'unrepresentative minority' spoiling a good-tempered protest. 'Some fools have just decided to spoil it for the rest of us,' claimed mature student Daniel Hamilton in *The Guardian* about the violence that followed the march. In doing so he identified a key issue at the heart of protest: what distinguishes a peaceful demonstration from direct action?

The Labour leader, Ed Miliband, commented that he was 'obviously' not in favour of violent

Figure 2.22 The demonstrations against tuition fees in 2010 were mostly peaceful ↑

protests but that he understood the depth of anger that people felt about rising tuition fees. He added, 'I applaud young people who peacefully demonstrate. I think peaceful demonstrations are part of our society.'

TUC march in March 2011

It is no more true to pretend that [the] TUC anti-cuts march changes everything than to pretend it changes nothing. The march through London was a very successful and impressive protest. A quarter to half of a million is a big turnout by any standards. There is also considerable polling evidence that it spoke, in general terms, for an increasingly large section of public opinion. To exaggerate the strength of the protest would be foolish – the public sector dominated TUC has not overnight become the voice of middle Britain. But it is even more foolish to dismiss the march as an event of no consequence.

The violence of a few hundred rioters should not cloud the issue. The overwhelming majority of marchers, Ed Miliband and the TUC included, were there to make a peaceful protest. Most of them only learned about the rioting when they got home. Unfortunately, there will always be a fringe who prefer to riot and they irresistibly attract the attention of the police and the television cameras.

But the government cannot simply pretend that there is nothing happening; it will have to respond. The TUC march was a success.

Source: adapted from *The Guardian* 2011

Figure 2.23 The majority of protestors at the TUC march in London, in March 2011, demonstrated peacefully against government cuts ↑

Government response

Michael Gove, Secretary of State for Education (speaking on the BBC Radio 4 *Today* programme), acknowledged the concerns of the demonstrators, but defended the implementation of the cuts, stating that 'we have to take steps to bring the public finances back into balance.'

Vince Cable, business secretary (speaking on the BBC 1 *Politics Show*), said that the government will not change its basic economic strategy as a result of the protest: 'No government – coalition, Labour or any other – would change its fundamental economic policy simply in response to a demonstration of that kind.'

The march took place only four months after the December 2010 student protests which focused on spending cuts and changes to higher and further education. Unfortunately a small minority of the demonstrators smashed shop windows and carried out other acts of vandalism. This demonstration has had no impact on the government plans to raise tuition fees to a maximum of £9000. However, the march did weaken the popularity of Nick Clegg, the Liberal Democrat leader who had promised, during the 2010 election campaign, not to raise tuition fees.

Gurkha Justice Campaign

Figure 2.24 Joanna Lumley with the Gurkha Justice Campaign ↑

After a high-profile campaign fronted by the actress Joanna Lumley, the Gurkha Justice Campaign inflicted an embarrassing Commons defeat on the government over the granting of rights of citizenship to former British soldiers. Below is part of the statement issued by Lumley on behalf of the campaigners:

> We simply would not have won this fight without the massive, overwhelming support of all those who supported the campaign. The hundreds of thousands of people who signed Gurkha Justice petitions, lobbied their MP, campaigned, attended rallies and marches – this is a victory. It would not have happened without them.
>
> The government has now responded to the campaign after votes in parliament, a huge media campaign and, most importantly, massive public support. I am delighted, and humbled, at what has been achieved.

Use of celebrities

Some pressure groups seek the support of celebrities in the hope of raising their profile. In 2011, many celebrities – including Naomi Campbell, Celine Dion, Annie Lennox, Scarlett Johansson and Davina McCall – lent their public support to the White Ribbon Alliance, pressurising the G8 to allocate money to help prevent women dying during childbirth.

How successful can pressure groups be?

It is very difficult to assess the effectiveness of pressure groups in influencing the legislative process and holding the Executive to account. Despite much publicity and both legal and illegal forms of direct action, students lost their battle to halt the trebling of English university tuition fees in 2011 after the government's legislation was passed by both houses.

Nevertheless, their action did have an impact on some backbench MPs – the government's margin of victory was reduced to 21 compared to an overall coalition majority of 84 – and they managed to dent the Liberal Democrats' self-image and public reputation. In the first by-election after the 2010 general election – Barnsley Central in 2011 – the Liberal Democrats slumped to sixth place, finishing behind the UK Independence Party, the British National Party and an independent as its share of the vote dropped to just over 4 per cent.

One student commented that after years in opposition, enjoying the luxury of consequence-free pandering to every pressure group that came to lobby them, Liberal Democrat MPs now knew the feeling of breaking pledges and having to trudge through the division lobbies to keep a government in power while police and protestors clashed in the streets outside.

Overall though, there are various factors that can determine how successful pressure groups can be. The most important are:

- core aims
- relationship with the government
- organisation, leadership and resources
- methods.

Core aims

A pressure group's success depends largely on whether or not they have empathy with the general public. If the public are sympathetic to their aims, their chances of success are increased. For example, after the Dunblane shootings in 1996 the Snowdrop Campaign had tremendous support from the public, and this put immense pressure on the government to ban the private ownership of handguns. The death of sixteen children and their teacher created an overwhelming public demand for the ban.

Relationship with the government

If the government recognises that a pressure group and its policies are compatible with its own views, then this will enhance the group's chance of success. Any direct contact with the government and decision makers behind the scenes is a crucial factor in determining the success of a pressure group (the BMA is an example of a pressure group with insider status).

Organisation, leadership and resources

How well organised the group is, and the articulation and skill of its leaders, is vital to achieving success. The amount of funds and resources available to the group can affect its chances of success. A well-financed group can afford to employ professional lobbyists and pay for advertising campaigns in the media.

Methods

The methods used will have an impact on success. Those refused insider status may choose other forms of direct action or civil disobedience. Their ability to use publicity through the media to forward their aims is also vital.

Are pressure groups a threat to democracy?

Pressure groups are often attacked for threatening the democratic process. It could be argued that any pressure on our elected representatives by external and minority interests threatens our whole democratic process.

Inequalities also exist between pressure groups. Wealthy, well-organised and well-connected groups and those able to inflict sanctions on the government by withdrawing their cooperation are more powerful and given more priority by the government. On the other hand, pressure groups do offer an invaluable contribution to enhancing democracy. Dealing as they often do with minority and specialised issues, they are a vital link between the public and the government. A major problem for the government is being able to reconcile the views and wishes of a population of over 60 million people with its own decisions. Therefore, to many people and groups – especially those who disagree with government decisions and the decision-making process – it must often seem that politicians and civil servants follow their own agenda without reference to their wishes.

On the whole, pressure groups are not policy or decision makers. Nevertheless, this does not exclude some insider groups from participating in the policy-making process. This is because they are a vital source of information and advice to the government. Therefore, many groups are often consulted early on in the process of policy formulation. However, some argue that these groups should not have such a privileged status and the power to influence the decision makers and policy formulation because they are not elected and so are not publicly accountable.

Pressure groups can enhance the democratic process:

- They can educate and inform the decision makers and the public on issues, and about each other's opinions and views.

- They can allow for participation between elections and represent those not of voting age.

- They allow for a wider spectrum of opinion than that represented by political parties.

- They allow for the expression of minority views.

- They can provide the expertise needed to help draft government legislation.

Pressure groups detract from the democratic process:

- The information they provide can be very biased, misleading and unreliable.

- The level of participation can be very low (members often just pay a membership fee).

- There are questions over the level of democracy within pressure groups.

- The actions of some pressure groups can have a disproportionate effect on decision makers.

- Direct action can be illegal and lead to mob rule.

- They can interfere with the normal process of representative democracy.

The influence of the media

The media can have an important role in both influencing the legislative process and holding the Executive and its members to account for their actions. (The influence of the media on voting behaviour is discussed on pages 33–37.)

The media has four main functions to perform:

- inform
- educate
- entertain
- advertise.

The UK has a long history of freedom of the press and broadcasting. Despite regular news bulletins, documentaries and educational programmes, television is mainly a medium designed to entertain the people. Because of its enormous power as a means of mass communication, television must accept legal restraints and must provide balance and neutrality in its broadcasts.

Failure to do this would result in a station's charter to broadcast being revoked. Newspapers have no such legal restraints, and can show political bias and favouritism towards a political party. Newspapers largely reflect the political opinions of their owners.

Television and radio

Television is a powerful medium for decision makers to communicate with the public. The live televised leaders' debates of 2010 allowed the main parties to reach voters in their own homes, with the result that 25 per cent of voters changed their minds on the way they were going to vote after the first contest (see pages 33–34). Headline stories in television news programmes like the main six and ten o'clock news can put the Executive under intense scrutiny. The same is true with more investigative programmes like *Newsnight*, *Panorama* and *Question Time*, where enormous pressure can be put on the Executive to account for their actions and policies.

This is also the case with radio. The *Today* programme on BBC Radio 4 is an early morning news and current affairs programme with almost 7 million regular listeners. It provides regular news bulletins, along with serious and often confrontational political interviews and in-depth reports.

Likewise, the *Jeremy Vine* show on Radio 2 has Jeremy Vine and guests discussing the news headlines and talking to the people making them. For example, in March 2011 the show discussed what David Cameron should do about the crisis in Libya. They began by highlighting the fact that the day before the show David Cameron had seemed ready to use military force to free Libya, while on the day of the show he was backtracking slightly. It included a report by political editor Nick Robinson, who examined what Libya revealed about the government's foreign policy and about the prime minister himself. Vine asked the question 'Has David Cameron's rhetoric been consistent in the Libya crisis?' He then invited the public to express what advice they would give to the prime minister on Libya by phoning 10 Downing Street on air.

Newspapers

Despite circulation falling by 22 per cent in the UK since 2007 (according to the Organisation for Economic Cooperation and Development), newspapers remain very important to MPs. They provide a form of opposition to, and scrutiny of, the government.

In 2011, business secretary Vince Cable was relieved of some of his powers after being recorded telling undercover *Daily Telegraph* reporters he had 'declared war' on Rupert Murdoch, the owner of News International (a group that includes *The Times*, *Sunday Times*, *The Sun* and *News of the World*). He claimed to have used his powers to block Murdoch's bid to take full control of BSkyB (see page 36). Media ownership has long been an area of political controversy – particularly when it involves Rupert Murdoch.

Table 2.7 **National Sunday newspapers: circulation between January 2010 and January 2011**

	January 2011	**January 2010**	**Change (%)**
*News of the World**	2,789,560	2,984,469	–6.53
Sunday Mirror	1,092,816	1,124,620	–2.83
The People	500,866	532,975	–6.02
Sunday Mail	366,325	395,126	–7.29
Daily Star Sunday	316,712	358,814	–11.73
Mail on Sunday	1,958,083	2,048,008	–4.39
Sunday Express	550,269	585,023	–5.94
Sunday Times	1,039,371	1,144,929	–9.22
Sunday Telegraph	496,128	527,742	–5.99
The Observer	314,164	354,565	–11.39
Independent on Sunday	152,561	153,975	–0.92

News of the World ended publication in July 2011

Source: www.guardian.co.uk

Figure 2.25 Rupert Murdoch, the owner of News International ↑

The Internet

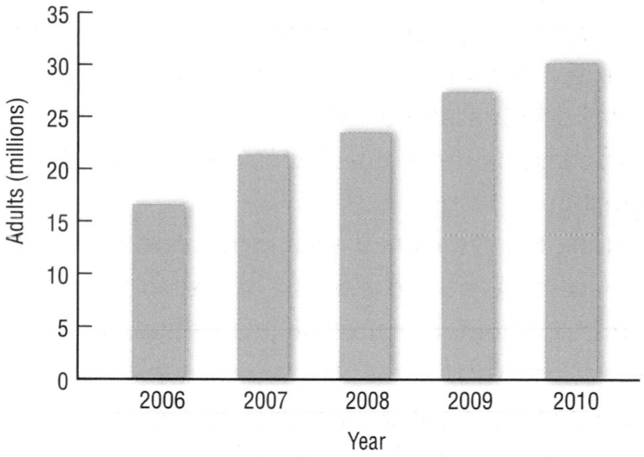

Figure 2.26 Adults accessing the Internet every day
Source: ONS Opinions Survey ↑

The thought of one man or company controlling a major part of the nation's newspaper and broadcasting interests is an issue of public concern – particularly when that person takes a close interest in the political agenda of their newspapers and one of them claims to influence general elections. Remember that famous headline 'It's the Sun Wot Won It', which appeared on the front page of *The Sun* in 1992 after it supported the Conservatives in the lead-up to their election victory?

It is generally accepted that freedom of speech is enhanced by having a diversity or plurality of media opinion. There are legal restrictions on media ownership, and major takeovers are subject to scrutiny by MPs and regulators.

The *Daily Telegraph* also secretly recorded Mr Cable claiming that he could 'bring the government down' by walking out of the coalition if 'pushed too far' in negotiations with Tory ministers, that being in the coalition government was 'like fighting a war' and that he could use the 'nuclear option' of quitting. The newspaper claimed a 'clear public interest' in defence of its actions.

The issue was eventually handed over to Jeremy Hunt, the culture and media secretary, to decide – but this was yet another government minister.

In 2010, 30.1 million adults in the UK (60 per cent) accessed the Internet every day or almost every day. This is nearly double the 2006 estimate of 16.5 million.

Watching television or listening to the radio over the Internet has been growing in popularity in recent years, with 17.4 million adults doing this in 2010 compared to 6.4 million in 2006.

Social networking was also a popular Internet activity in 2010, with 43 per cent of Internet users posting messages to social networking sites or chat sites, blogs, etc. Social networking proved to be most popular among 16 to 24 year olds, with 75 per cent posting messages; meanwhile, 50 per cent of this age group uploaded self-created content. However, social networking is not limited to young adults: 31 per cent of Internet users aged 45 to 54 had used the Internet to post messages, while 28 per cent had uploaded content.

There were 19.2 million households with an Internet connection in 2010, representing 73 per cent of households.

Even the prime minister has an official website: www.number10.gov.uk. He claims to be using it in an attempt to make the government more open and transparent. On the site, the government have published a huge amount of information about the inner workings of government and request comments on how they can do things better – both in terms of what they publish and how they're going about it. They have even set up a link for feedback (http://transparency.number10.gov.uk).

Also, the public can both create and sign petitions on this website. No longer does anyone need to visit 10 Downing Street to hand over a petition; e-petitions give more people the opportunity to deliver a petition directly to Downing Street.

Below is an extract from an e-petition demanding government intervention in the Edinburgh trams issue.

E-petition: Edinburgh trams

We the undersigned petition the prime minister to intervene in the matter of the Edinburgh tram project.

I implore the prime minister or Government to intervene with regards to the subject of the Edinburgh tram system. Due to the incompetence of the senior level management, the immediate necessity has arisen for the prime minister or Government to intervene and assume control of the project or to appoint a replacement contractor to continue the works at the negligible cost and timeframe previously agreed.

Source: adapted from www.number10.gov.uk

Since February 2011, voters have had the opportunity to give their views on legislation. The move follows a coalition government commitment to 'introduce a new public reading stage for bills to give the public an opportunity to comment on proposed legislation online'.

The Protection of Freedoms Bill was the first piece of legislation to be put online as part of the coalition's plan to involve the wider public in the legislative process. Ministers want MPs to take into account the views posted on the public reading stage website (http://publicreadingstage.cabinetoffice.gov.uk) when they debate any bill. David Cameron commented:

Right now a tiny percentage of the population write legislation that will apply to 100 per cent of the population. This makes our laws poorer because it shuts out countless people across the country whose expertise could help. And it makes our politics poorer because it increases the sense that parliament is somehow separate from the people rather than subservient to them. Our new public reading stage will improve the level of debate and scrutiny of bills by giving everyone the opportunity to go online and offer their views on any new legislation. That will mean better laws – and more trust in our politics.

Source: www.cabinetoffice.gov.uk/news/big-society-opening-parliament-people

Freedom of Information Act

The Freedom of Information Act became law in 2005, making government more open and accessible and also more transparent and accountable. The act allows any person to request and receive information from a public body, subject to certain exemptions. These public bodies include central government departments and agencies, local councils, the NHS (including health authorities and hospital trusts), the police, and state schools, colleges and universities.

These public bodies have to release information unless it is covered by either a qualified or absolute exemption. Qualified exemptions are enforced if it is in the public interest to keep something secret – for example, information that would prejudice the formulation of government policy, the effective conduct of public affairs, national security or international relations.

Freedom of information can be a useful tool for the media to obtain factual background material relating to government policy decisions and legislation. It can also be used to hold the Executive and its members to account and shed light on the decision-making process and generate news stories, by revealing material that would otherwise have remained secret.

For this reason pressure groups and the media have been active users of the legislation, as have the general public. For example, it led to details of MPs' expenses being put into the public domain. Details of claims under the second-homes allowance used to be kept secret, but Freedom of Information campaigners won a High Court case to get them released after years of battling with the House of Commons.

The pressure group Republic, which campaigns for a democratic alternative to the monarchy, is attempting to have the exemption of the royal household from the act removed to allow more transparency and make it more publicly accountable. They say 'the continued secrecy surrounding the palace and Clarence House is simply unacceptable in a modern democracy … The people have the same right to access information from the palace as they do from government.' Republic staged a protest outside Buckingham Palace against royal secrecy in March 2011.

This extra scrutiny tool of the media and pressure groups has resulted in the government fighting back with attempts to discourage its use, at times trying to spoil newspaper scoops by posting replies to requests online – therefore making them available to all journalists, rather than only to those who had taken the trouble to make the request.

Activities

1 Explain, in your own words, what a pressure group is.

2 Explain what is meant by cause and interest groups.

3 What is the difference between an outsider and an insider pressure group?

4 Describe, in detail, the three roles of pressure groups in the UK today.

5 Describe the main methods used by pressure groups.

6 Describe the factors that can determine how successful pressure groups can be.

7 What functions do the media perform?

8 Describe, in detail and with examples, how television and radio can put the Executive under scrutiny.

9 What is the public reading stage in the UK legislative process?

10 How can the Freedom of Information Act be used to hold the Executive to account?

Past exam questions

1 Assess the effectiveness of pressure groups in influencing decision making in central government.

2 Pressure groups are a threat to democracy. Discuss.

Devolved decision making in Scotland

Scottish devolution and electoral systems

Introduction

In 1707, the Act of Union brought to an end the existence of separate parliaments in Scotland and England. In their place it created one single parliament at Westminster in London.

Almost 300 years later and 800 years after William Wallace defeated the English at the Battle of Stirling Bridge, a referendum was held on proposals for a directly elected Scottish Parliament with wide legislative powers. On 11 September 1997, these proposals received overwhelming support from the people of Scotland. The turnout was 60.4 per cent, with 74.3 per cent voting in favour of a Scottish Parliament and 60.2 per cent for the parliament to have tax-varying powers. This result was enough for Prime Minister Tony Blair to say, 'This is a good day for Scotland, and a good day for Britain and the United Kingdom … the era of big centralised government is over.'

The following year, the Scotland Act (1998) cleared a pathway for the creation once again of a Scottish Parliament with the power to pass laws affecting Scotland in a variety of areas, known as devolved matters. The first elections for the Scottish Parliament were held on 6 May 1999, and the first meeting of the Scottish Parliament took place on 12 May 1999. On 1 July 1999, the Scottish Parliament was officially opened by Her Majesty the Queen and received its full legislative powers.

The first words in the Scotland Act (1998) were brought to fruition: 'There shall be a Scottish Parliament.' However, this Act is to be amended by the Scotland Bill (2010–11) (see page 96).

Figure 3.1 The Scottish Parliament ↑

Devolution

Devolution is the transfer of powers from a central body to devolved administrations. In the UK, some powers have been transferred from the UK Parliament at Westminster to various nations and regions. For example, different powers have been devolved to the Scottish Parliament, the National Assembly for Wales and the Northern Ireland Assembly. There are also levels of devolution in London and plans for further devolution to English regional assemblies.

Consequently, the people of Scotland have their own parliament where, under the terms of the Scotland Act (1998), they are free to pass laws on a range of issues and have the power to raise or lower the basic rate of income tax by up to 3 pence in the pound.

In Scotland, devolved matters include education and health (the NHS in Scotland). The Scotland Act also specifies other matters on which the Scottish Parliament cannot pass legislation; these are known as reserved matters and include defence and national security (see page 80). Despite this degree of self-government for specific countries and regions, the UK Government still has overall or absolute power and can reverse the devolved settlements at any time.

The UK now has three Executives, with devolved powers for 16.4 per cent of the population and one government for England and the UK.

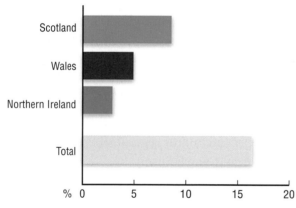

Figure 3.2 **Percentage of UK population of countries with their own Executive** ↑

What is the difference between the Scottish Parliament and the Scottish Government?

The Scottish Parliament and the Scottish Government are often mistakenly taken to mean the same thing. However, it is important to recognise that they are different and separate organisations.

The Scottish Parliament is made up of 129 MSPs, who are elected by the people of Scotland. The Scottish Parliament is the law-making body in Scotland for devolved matters, in the same way that the UK Parliament legislates on reserved matters. It also scrutinises the work of the Scottish Government.

The Scottish Government is a separate organisation from the Scottish Parliament, with a different role and function. It is responsible for formulating and implementing policy on the devolved matters. The members of the Scottish Government are collectively referred to as 'the Scottish Ministers'; all ministers have to be MSPs, except the lord advocate and the solicitor general.

However, the relationship is one of interdependence: the government derives legitimacy from parliament, and parliament relies on the government to take care of the business of government and administration.

The Scottish Parliament

- is made up of 129 MSPs

- elects a presiding officer, who chairs meetings of the parliament and represents parliament externally

- is the law-making body in Scotland for devolved matters and scrutinises the work of the Scottish Government

- is located in Holyrood, at the foot of the Royal Mile.

The Scottish Government

- is normally formed from the party holding most seats in the Scottish Parliament

- is led by the first minister and comprises cabinet secretaries and ministers chosen by the first minister

- is responsible for developing and implementing policy on devolved matters

- is located in buildings across Scotland, with its main offices in central Edinburgh and Glasgow.

Devolved and reserved matters

Only some issues can be dealt with by the Scottish Parliament. These are known as devolved matters because the power to make laws in these areas has been devolved (transferred) from Westminster and the UK Parliament.

The devolved matters

The Scotland Act (1998) does not set out devolved matters but instead lists 'reserved matters' for which the UK Parliament retains responsibility. By definition, devolved matters on which the parliament can legislate are all those which are not specifically reserved. Devolved matters include:

- health
- education and training
- local government
- social work
- housing
- planning
- tourism, economic development and financial assistance to industry
- some aspects of transport, including the Scottish road network, bus policy, and ports and harbours
- law and home affairs
- the police and fire services
- the environment
- natural and built heritage
- agriculture, forestry and fishing
- sport and the arts
- statistics, public registers and records.

The reserved matters

The UK Parliament continues to legislate for Scotland on reserved matters. It may also legislate on devolved matters in Scotland. Reserved matters include:

- constitutional matters
- UK foreign policy

Figure 3.3 Nuclear energy is one of the UK Parliament's reserved matters ↑

- UK defence and national security
- the fiscal, economic and monetary system
- immigration and nationality
- energy: electricity, coal, gas and nuclear energy
- common markets
- trade and industry, including competition and customer protection
- some aspects of transport, including railways, transport safety and regulation
- employment legislation
- social security
- gambling and the National Lottery
- data protection
- equal opportunities.

Founding principles of the Scottish Parliament

The Scottish Parliament has four founding principles that aim to create an effective and accountable parliament, answering the needs of the people of Scotland. The four principles are:

- sharing power
- accountability
- accessibility, openness and participation
- equal opportunities.

These mean that:

- The Scottish Parliament should embody and reflect the sharing of power between the people of Scotland, the legislators and the Scottish Government.
- The Scottish Government should be accountable to the Scottish Parliament, and the Parliament and Government should be accountable to the people of Scotland.
- The Scottish Parliament should be accessible, open and responsive; it should develop procedures that make possible a participative approach to the development, consideration and scrutiny of policy and legislation.
- The Scottish Parliament in its operation and its appointments should recognise the need to promote equal opportunities for all.

The Scottish Parliament has put in place procedures to ensure it lives up to these four founding principles. These include the following:

- the committee system
- the legislative process
- the electoral system
- other features (such as question time).

Committees

The Scottish Parliament's committee system allows for accessibility, openness and participation. It is generally accepted that the real work of the parliament is done in committee rooms.

Every piece of legislation coming out of Holyrood will have come under the scrutiny of one or more of the Scottish Parliament's committees. Out of the three stages in the passage of a bill, the legislation is scrutinised by a committee at two of them (stages 1 and 2) before the whole parliament debates and votes whether to pass it at stage 3. (See Figure 3.7.)

But what makes the committee system at Holyrood even more open and accessible is the fact that it allows for the participation of as many people as possible in the democratic process. Committees normally meet in public and can do so anywhere in Scotland, not just inside parliament. Since the Scottish Parliament was established in 1999, around 100 committee meetings have been held outside Edinburgh. In fact, most committees allow the general public to attend – some argue that this is true democracy in action.

Fact File

External committee meetings in 2010

Figure 3.4 The Public Petitions Committee meeting at Waid Academy, Anstruther ↑

- The Public Petitions Committee met in Arran High School, Lamlash, Arran, in September 2010 and in Waid Academy, Anstruther, in March 2010.
- The Equal Opportunities Committee met in the City Chambers, Glasgow, in June 2010.
- The Health and Sport Committee met in the Macdonald Loch Rannoch Hotel, Kinloch Rannoch, in January 2010.

This reflects the greater importance and influence of committees in the Scottish Parliament compared to its counterpart in

Westminster. This is the case because, unlike Westminster, the Scottish Parliament is a single-chamber parliament; it has no upper house or second chamber (like the House of Lords), meaning that the whole process of passing legislation is different.

This situation gives committees significant strength in influencing decision making in the Scottish Parliament. Committees undertake pre-legislative scrutiny of every scrap of proposed legislation, and most amendments to bills are made during committee meetings. Therefore, it is through the function of committees that the Scottish Government is held to account by the parliament.

Gathering evidence and information

Most of the work of committees comprises the gathering and recording of evidence and information. This can be done in several ways; for example, witnesses can give evidence in person or by letter or email – even by video conference, especially if it is difficult for them to travel. This work is mainly carried out when committees have to:

- scrutinise the activities of the Scottish Government
- scrutinise a proposal or draft bill
- investigate a matter
- decide whether to propose a committee bill
- consider a bill
- consider proposals for members' bills
- consider and report on subordinate legislation.

Membership

Committee membership is restricted to MSPs who are not in the government. Most have eight members, but they are allowed to have between five and fifteen. The appointment of members takes account of the balance of the various political parties and groupings in the parliament, with all MSPs normally being on at least one committee but occasionally two.

The Parliamentary Bureau can also recommend changes to the membership or make-up of committees.

> **The Parliamentary Bureau is a group of MSPs representing political parties and groupings with five or more MSPs in the parliament. They meet regularly to discuss the parliament's business and propose its business programme.**

All committees are chaired by a convener and meet regularly – either weekly or fortnightly, depending on their workload. The members of the committee choose a convener from a political party decided by parliament following a recommendation by the Parliamentary Bureau (based on party numbers in parliament). In addition, each committee normally has a deputy convener who will chair meetings in the convener's absence. Deputy conveners are chosen in the same way as conveners. These are important roles because conveners can set the committee agenda, steering what is discussed and – sometimes more importantly – what is not discussed.

Ordinary committee members can raise issues during meetings and get their concerns recorded. They can also attend and speak at any committee meetings, including those they are not a member of, but they can only vote in their own committees.

Because of the strength of party discipline committee members usually follow their party line, but there is sometimes a conflict of interest between their constituents' views, their party and their own personal interests.

Nevertheless, of the fifteen committees (eight mandatory and seven subject) in the parliament of 2007–11 the convenership was as follows: five were led by the SNP, five by Labour, two by the Conservatives, two by the Liberal Democrats and one by the Green Party.

The system has the potential to be used by opposition parties to push through their own legislation or publish critical reports on the government. Still, as one Green MSP and convener of the committee dealing with climate change put it, 'Members of the committees must strive to work constructively, putting the interests of the country, and, in this case, the planet, before short-term political objectives.'

The parliament has different kinds of committees. Under parliamentary rules, it must establish mandatory committees. There are currently eight mandatory committees, including the Public Petitions Committee and the Equal Opportunities Committee. It can also set up subject committees to look at specific subjects or areas of policy. There are currently seven subject committees that reflect the cabinet secretary portfolios. These include the Health and Sport Committee and the Education, Lifelong Learning and Culture Committee. However, the parliament can also establish temporary committees on a short-term basis to consider particular issues. These include private bill committees, which are established to consider a particular bill that has been introduced by a person or body who is not an MSP.

Functions of committees

Committees have two key functions: to scrutinise the work of the Scottish Government and to examine legislation. Their work involves the following three main areas.

Legislation

Committees can consider and amend proposals for new laws. They can also propose new laws themselves in the form of committee bills.

Inquiries

Committees can investigate any area that is within their remit and affects the people of Scotland, and can publish a report setting out their recommendations. Past inquiry reports have included youth justice and eating disorders. These reports are normally discussed at a meeting of the full parliament, and as a consequence have influenced government policies and resulted in changes to legislation.

Other areas

Committees can also consider and report on government policy and actions, on European legislation, on secondary (or subordinate) legislation and on public petitions concerning the people of Scotland.

Mandatory committees

- Audit
- Equal Opportunities
- European and External Relations
- Finance
- Public Petitions
- Standards, Procedures and Public Appointments
- Subordinate Legislation
- Procedures

Subject committees

- Economy, Energy and Tourism
- Education, Lifelong Learning and Culture
- Health and Sport
- Justice
- Local Government and Communities
- Rural Affairs and Environment
- Transport, Infrastructure and Climate Change

Public Petitions Committee

The Public Petitions Committee considers petitions that have been submitted to the Scottish Parliament, and may decide to refer them to other committees for further consideration. Petitions are submitted by individuals and groups who want to raise an issue. The public petitions system is a key part of the Scottish Parliament's commitment to openness and accessibility. All committees have a responsibility to consider and report on any petitions referred to them by the Public Petitions Committee. Petitions can have positive outcomes that lead to change or inform debate. For example, they can:

- lead to changes in law
- be considered as part of a wider inquiry
- initiate parliamentary debates
- prompt action from the Scottish Government or another public body
- inform the scrutiny of legislation
- result in changes to regulations and guidance.

What can committees do?

Committees can:

- **decide their own priorities independent of government**

- **look at the bills proposed by the government**

- **look at the need for new legislation and conduct inquiries**

- **propose their own bills to parliament**

- **look at members' bills**

- **look at petitions referred to them by the Petitions Committee**

- **monitor legislation to see if it is working properly**

- **question ministers, quangos and civil servants**

- **consult organisations and individuals**

- **consider financial proposals and the financial administration of the Scottish administration**

- **hold debates in the chamber (each committee is allotted chamber time).**

Legislation

A major role of any parliament is to make laws. The Scottish Parliament, in line with its founding principles, involves the whole people of Scotland along with regional and interested organisations, pressure groups and individuals, ensuring a high degree of accessibility and openness. This allows for a level of participation and the sharing of power that helps avoid a situation where the Executive can dominate the legislative process completely. Instead, provision is made for individual MSPs and committees to introduce or propose legislation as well as the Executive. In effect, this provides a realistic opportunity for the people of Scotland to influence new laws and drive it towards the aim of being a people's parliament by the sharing of power between the people of Scotland, the legislators and the Scottish Executive, and being accessible, open and responsive. It also makes possible a participative approach to the development, consideration and scrutiny of legislation.

Before they become Acts of the Scottish Parliament, legislative proposals are known as bills. A bill becomes an Act by being passed by the parliament and receiving royal assent.

Pre-legislative consultation

Before any legislative proposal becomes a bill it goes through a pre-legislative consultation process. This whole process is designed to allow for maximum participation in an open and accessible manner. For example, with an executive bill the relevant minister informs the relevant committee of the proposed legislation and recommends which relevant groups or individuals should be involved in the pre-legislative consultation process. The Executive then consults the relevant bodies, identifying any issues of concern. In addition, the relevant committee is kept informed throughout. When the process is completed and the draft bill is introduced, the outcome of the consultation process is attached to it as a memorandum – ensuring openness from the start.

Types of bill

There are two different types of bill that can be introduced: a public bill and a private bill.

All public bills are introduced by MSPs in the parliament. They may be introduced by members of the Scottish Government as an executive bill, by one of the parliament's committees as a committee bill or by an individual MSP as a members' bill.

A private bill can be introduced by an individual or group of people.

Figure 3.5 Patricia Ferguson MSP speaking in the Scottish Parliament during the Stage 1 Debate: Local Electoral Administration ↑

Executive bills

These are bills introduced by the Scottish Executive, and they account for the majority of legislation. Between 2003 and 2007, executive bills accounted for 70 per cent of all legislation introduced, with a success rate in achieving royal assent of 87 per cent.

Alcohol Etc. (Scotland) Bill

Purpose of the bill

To make provision regulating the sale of alcohol and the licensing of premises on which alcohol is sold.

Passage of the bill

The bill was introduced in the parliament by Nicola Sturgeon MSP on 25 November 2009.

The bill passed stage 1 on 10 June 2010.

Stage 2 was completed on 5 October 2010.

The stage 3 debate was held on 10 November 2010, and the bill passed stage 3 on the same day.

The bill received royal assent on 15 December 2010.

Other executive bills include the Schools (Health Promotion and Nutrition) (Scotland) Bill and the Custodial Sentences and Weapons (Scotland) Bill.

Committee bills

Committees can make their own proposals for legislation in the form of committee bills. The legislative process is slightly different from that of executive bills, which are introduced by the Scottish Government. Between 2003 and 2007, only one committee bill was introduced; it was successfully passed and received royal assent.

The Commissioner for Children and Young People (Scotland) Bill created the post of commissioner for children and young people in Scotland, with the general function of promoting and safeguarding the rights of children and young people. See www.scottish.parliament.uk/business/bills/billsPassed/b71s1.pdf.

Figure 3.6 Tam Baillie, Scotland's commissioner for children and young people ←

When the first committee bill was passed by the parliament, Alasdair Morgan MSP, then convener of the Justice Committee, said: 'The ability of Scottish Parliament committees to initiate legislation is an important part of what makes our system of governance innovative and fundamentally different from Westminster.'

Members' bills

Any MSP who is not a member of the Executive can introduce a members' bill. They have the right to lodge up to two members' bills per parliamentary session. Around a quarter of all bills introduced between 2003 and 2007 were members' bills, with a success rate in achieving royal assent of 11 per cent.

Private bills

Private bills differ slightly from public bills and are subject to different procedures.

A private bill is introduced by what is known as a promoter. A promoter can be an individual person, a group of people or a company; therefore, these are sometimes known as 'personal bills'. Generally they relate to development projects or changes to the use of land.

Between 2003 and 2007, private bills accounted for 11 per cent of all bills introduced with a success rate in achieving royal assent of around 80 per cent. All private bills are subject to a three-stage process.

- Preliminary stage: a Private Bill Committee is established to agree on the general principles of the bill.
- Consideration stage: committee members consider the detail of the bill.
- Final stage: parliament debates the bill and a vote is taken to pass it or not.
- Royal assent: the bill becomes an Act.

One successful private bill was the Glasgow Airport rail link bill, which gave powers to the Strathclyde Passenger Transport Executive (Strathclyde Partnership for Transport) to construct a new railway service between Glasgow Airport and Glasgow Central Station. It completed the final stage, was approved by MSPs in November 2006 and received royal assent in January 2007. Unfortunately, the SNP minority government cancelled the project in 2010 as a result of the recession.

The majority of bills introduced and passed are executive bills. This is because the Executive can usually rely on an overall majority of MSPs to support it. Most parties use a 'whip system' to ensure party unity in voting. The SNP minority government of 2007–11 had to negotiate with the other parties to try to get its legislation passed. The SNP government of 2011–16, with its majority in parliament, has not faced the same problems.

With members' bills, individual MSPs must get cross-party support and have more limited resources to support them.

Committees and legislation

Bills need to complete three stages to become an Act of the Scottish Parliament. Committees are heavily involved from the beginning of the legislative process through to scrutinising proposed legislation.

Stage 1: general principles (committee)

The bill is referred to the committee with the relevant subject remit, known as the lead committee. Other committees can also consider and report their views to the lead committee. In addition, the lead committee must take account of any views submitted to it by the Finance Committee. The lead committee will make recommendations about whether parliament should agree to the bill's general principles.

Stage 2: detailed consideration (committee)

If parliament agrees to the general principles of the bill at stage 1, it then proceeds to stage 2. Here it will receive more detailed, line-by-line scrutiny by the lead committee. The committee will also consider any proposed amendments put forward by MSPs and will decide which amendments to accept. At this stage, the committee can also take further evidence.

Stage 3: further detailed consideration (parliament)

If the bill proceeds to stage 3, the whole parliament will then consider and vote on whether to pass it in its amended and final form. If parliament passes the bill it goes forward for royal assent, becoming an Act of the Scottish Parliament.

Business

Adapted from the Scottish Parliament public information service.

Debating chamber: an arena for conflict, cooperation and decision making

The debating chamber is the focal point for the Scottish Parliament's business. It is here that all 129 MSPs come together to debate issues and decide on new laws. It is also where MSPs question the first minister, cabinet secretaries and ministers, and where statements are made on policy developments and key events.

The Parliamentary Bureau is responsible for the allocation of time in the chamber.

The government gets most of the debating time, while time is allocated to the opposition parties in proportion to the number of seats they hold in the parliament.

In addition, opposition parties can choose the topic on sixteen half-sitting days and committees on twelve days in each parliamentary year.

Table 3.1 Bills by type and outcome, 2003–7 (as at 26 March 2007)

Type of bill	Number	Royal assent	Success rate (%)
Executive	53	46	87
Committee	1	1	100
Members'	18	2	11
Private	9	7	80
Total	81	56	69

Source: Scottish Parliament

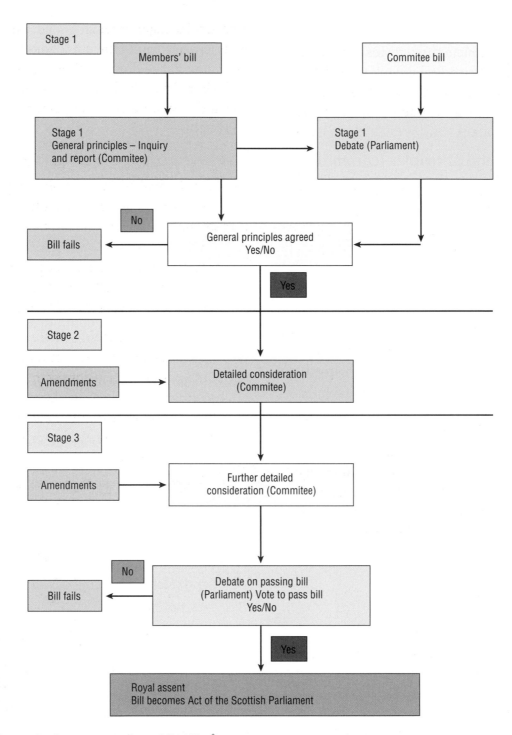

Figure 3.7 Stages in the passage of a public bill ⬆

Debates

Debates allow MSPs to discuss topical issues. They are usually based on a motion, which is a proposal that the parliament should do something or express an opinion about an issue. Cabinet secretaries or ministers and the party spokespersons on the issue generally give a speech to open and then close a debate. During the debate, MSPs can suggest amendments to a motion and they can ask the person who is speaking if he or she will 'give way' or 'take an intervention', allowing them to ask a question or make an observation.

Voting on motions

If amendments have been suggested to a motion, MSPs vote on these before deciding on the motion itself. If any amendment is accepted, MSPs then take a vote on the 'motion as amended'. A motion that has been agreed by the parliament is called a resolution.

At decision time, the presiding officer goes through the list of motions and amendments that have been considered that day and, for each one, asks MSPs if they all agree with what is being proposed. If any MSP answers 'no', the presiding officer announces that there will be a division (a vote). MSPs can vote 'yes', 'no' or 'abstain' by pressing the appropriate voting button on the electronic consoles on their desks. After the 30-second voting period has ended, the computer system calculates the result and it is announced by the presiding officer.

Members' business

Members' business is a debate on a motion proposed by an individual MSP who is not a cabinet secretary or minister. It allows individual MSPs to influence the decision-making process by highlighting an issue of concern to their constituents or of interest to themselves or a particular region that might not otherwise receive attention. Members' business normally takes place after decision time on Wednesdays and Thursdays, and lasts up to 45 minutes. It concludes without any vote being taken.

Parliamentary questions

Parliamentary questions are one of the ways in which individual MSPs can hold the government to account and provide a means for them to extract factual and statistical information. However, it is frowned upon if MSPs try to use a question to make a political statement.

There are several different ways that MSPs can ask questions in the Scottish Parliament.

First minister's question time

Every Thursday for up to 30 minutes, MSPs can ask questions of the first minister in the chamber. Six questions are selected by the presiding officer and these are published in the business bulletin, normally on the Tuesday before they will be asked in the chamber.

Figure 3.8 First minister's question time ↑

General question time and themed question time

One day each week for up to twenty minutes, MSPs can ask general questions of the cabinet secretaries and ministers. At the same time there is also a 40-minute period set aside for questions on specified themes such as health or education. These themes change each week.

Emergency questions

Emergency questions allow MSPs to get information and comment on a matter of immediate concern. The answers are given by the relevant minister, or law officer, or the first minister. For example, in September 2010 Bill Butler MSP asked the minister for public health and sport an emergency question about the welfare of Scottish athletes participating in the Commonwealth Games in Delhi. Ten minutes were allowed for the question and any supplementary questions.

Questions following a ministerial statement

Ministerial statements inform parliament about urgent or topical issues. For example, statements have been made on the future of Scottish higher education, severe weather and the strategic defence review. Normally, a cabinet secretary or minister delivers a statement for between ten and fifteen minutes without interruption, and then answers questions on it from MSPs for around twenty minutes.

Legislative consent motion (formerly Sewel motion)

Prior to 30 November 2005, this type of motion was known as a Sewel motion.

While the Scottish Parliament legislates for Scotland on devolved matters, the UK Parliament at Westminster continues to legislate for Scotland on reserved matters. However, in certain circumstances the Scottish Parliament may give its consent for Westminster to legislate for Scotland on devolved matters. This procedure is known as a legislative consent motion.

Legislative consent motions are generally used when:

- it makes sense to legislate on a UK-wide basis
- it will save legislative time in the Scottish Parliament
- legislating at Westminster could be an appropriate means of dealing with issues that straddle both devolved and reserved matters
- an operational role is proposed for Scottish ministers in reserved areas.

Between 1999 and 2011 there were 112 legislative consent motions in areas such as climate change, serious crime, immigration, adoption and children. Most are related to the justice and security areas.

Today there are conflicting views over the use of these motions. One view is that they diminish the importance of the Scottish Parliament and the democratic process; the other is that they operate to the benefit of the people of Scotland. Under the Sewel Convention, Westminster will not pass bills that contain relevant provisions without first obtaining the consent of the Scottish Parliament. The consent itself is given through a motion (a legislative consent motion), which is taken in the chamber – but the detailed scrutiny is undertaken by a Scottish Parliament committee on the basis of a memorandum. Critics argue that the Scottish Government is using Westminster to legislate on controversial issues and bypassing the debate of contentious issues in the Scottish Parliament through their use.

The Scottish Executive

'There shall be a Scottish Executive' (paragraph 44 of the Scotland Act (1998)).

The Scottish Executive is the government in Scotland for devolved matters, and is responsible for formulating and implementing policy in these areas.

Tension between constituency and list MSPs

One consequence of the electoral system is that the traditional link between constituents and their representatives is now more complex. The constituency MSP represents a specific area and, having defeated other party candidates in a straightforward first past the post contest, he or she can claim to be the 'people's choice'. In the 2011 elections Derek Mackay, SNP, was elected as the constituency MSP for North and West Renfrewshire. However, voters in North and West Renfrewshire are also represented by seven list MSPs. Among those seven is Annabel Goldie, then leader of the Scottish Conservative Party. As a former leader of a political party, Annabel Goldie has a far higher profile than Derek Mackay. Constituents in North and West Renfrewshire can contact either Derek Mackay or any of the seven list MSPs, including Annabel Goldie.

Both constituency and list MSPs complain about each other's actions. Constituency MSPs are convinced that list MSPs 'cherry pick' local issues and conduct electioneering with the purpose of winning the seat at a future election. In contrast, list MSPs argue that constituency MSPs regard them as second-class politicians. It is significant that much of the criticism of list MSPs comes from Labour MSPs. Labour tends to do better in first past the post constituency elections and resents list MSPs who failed to win under first past the post. In 2003 the then Labour MP Brian Wilson controversially stated that 'list MSPs were underemployed wastes of space'.

In the 2011 election Labour's failure to place its heavyweight constituency candidates onto the list system as a safety net had disastrous consequences (see pages 11–14).

However, after the Scottish parliamentary elections of 2007 the new SNP administration announced that the Scottish Executive was to be renamed and rebranded as the Scottish Government. While this is now the case, the name 'Scottish Executive' is still the legal name because any change must come about with an amendment to the Scotland Act. This can only be done by Westminster and not by the wishes of the first minister, the Scottish Executive or Scottish Parliament. This change may be seen as driving a wedge between Scotland and the rest of the UK to emphasise the two separate institutions of government.

Nevertheless, the original symbol of the Scottish Executive – the royal arms for Scotland and the words 'The Scottish Executive' (in both English and Gaelic) – has been replaced with the flag of Scotland and the words 'The Scottish Government'.

The Scottish Government is led by the first minister, who is nominated by the parliament and appointed by the Queen. He or she in turn appoints Scottish ministers to make up a cabinet, but only with the agreement of parliament and the approval of the monarch. However, the SNP initiated a further change to names in 2007 by introducing the term cabinet secretary in place of minister.

Choosing the first minister and the Executive

After a Scottish parliamentary election, a first minister is formally nominated by the parliament before being officially appointed by the monarch on the advice of the presiding officer. The Scottish Parliament has 28 days in which to nominate one of its members for appointment as first minister, who in turn appoints the Scottish ministers to make up his or her cabinet with the agreement of parliament and the approval of the Queen.

In the 2007–11 parliament, the first minister of Scotland was Alex Salmond of the SNP. He made political history after becoming the first nationalist to be elected first minister of Scotland. He was voted into office by parliament after seeing off a final challenge from Scottish Labour leader Jack McConnell by 49 votes to 46. He was supported by the Greens while the Liberal Democrats and Conservatives abstained. In May 2011, Alex Salmond was the only candidate for the post of first minister.

Figure 3.9 Alex Salmond was re-elected first minister in May 2011 ↑

The first minister is the head of the devolved Scottish Government. He or she leads the Scottish cabinet and is responsible for the development, implementation and presentation of government policy, constitutional affairs, and promoting and representing Scotland. The first minister is also directly accountable to the Scottish Parliament for his or her actions and the actions of the Scottish Government.

There is no fixed term of office for the first minister, unlike the four-year maximum term for members of the Scottish Parliament. Instead, after appointment the first minister can remain in position until he or she resigns, is dismissed or dies. There have only been four first ministers in the short history of the Scottish Parliament: the first, Donald Dewar, died in office and the second, Henry McLeish, resigned. In both of these circumstances, it was the responsibility of the presiding officer to appoint someone to serve as first minister in the interim, until the Scottish Parliament decided on a new nominee to be presented to the monarch for formal appointment. The third, Jack McConnell, left office after the 2007 election that saw the SNP become the biggest party in the parliament. Alex Salmond is the fourth and current first minister.

The term 'Scottish ministers' collectively refers to the first minister, the cabinet secretaries, the lord advocate and the solicitor general, who together make up the Scottish Government. Each cabinet secretary is responsible for a particular department and will indicate to the parliament what actions his or her department intends to take, and what legislation it wants the parliament to agree to. The Executive is accountable to the parliament for its actions.

In the 2007–11 parliament, the SNP formed a single-party minority Scottish Government. After the May 2007 elections, they emerged as the largest single party in the Scottish Parliament with the most seats: 47 of the 129 available. In the 2011–16 Scottish Parliament the SNP had the majority of seats: 69 of the 129 available.

The 2007–11 SNP government was the first minority administration since devolution and began a new form of consensus and inclusive politics in Scotland. Salmond's government had to seek parliament's approval 'policy by policy'

Table 3.2 Scotland's first ministers, 1999–2011

First minister	Term of office	Reason for end of office
Donald Dewar	May 1999–October 2000	Died
Henry McLeish	October 2000–November 2001	Resigned
Jack McConnell	November 2001–May 2007	Lost election
Alex Salmond	May 2007–May 2011 May 2011–	

Figure 3.10 Scotland's four first ministers: Donald Dewar, Henry McLeish, Jack McConnell and Alex Salmond ↑

across the chamber. This made it difficult for the SNP to achieve its goals, one of which was to hold a referendum on Scottish independence.

The lord advocate (the chief legal officer of the Scottish Government) and the solicitor general are members of the Scottish Executive, as set out in the Scotland Act (1998). However, after becoming first minister Alex Salmond decided that the lord advocate should no longer attend the Scottish cabinet, stating that he wished to 'de-politicise the post'.

The Scottish Government is responsible for devolved matters, most of which affect the day-to-day lives of the people of Scotland – for example, health, education, justice, rural affairs and transport.

It manages an annual budget of around £30 billion and each cabinet secretary is responsible for a particular department. Ministers are therefore part of two separate organisations: the Scottish Executive (as cabinet secretaries or ministers) and the Scottish Parliament (as MSPs). In addition to a constituency or regional office dealing with local matters, they may also have a ministerial office within a Scottish Executive building dealing with ministerial responsibilities.

The term 'Scottish Government' is also used as a collective term to describe Scottish ministers, including civil servants. Civil servants in Scotland must remain politically neutral and are accountable to Scottish ministers, who are themselves accountable to the Scottish Parliament. The Scottish Government and the Scottish Parliament are accountable to the people of Scotland.

The Scottish cabinet

The Scottish cabinet usually meets on a weekly basis, but only while parliament is sitting. It consists of the first minister and other Scottish ministers (cabinet secretaries), excluding the Scottish law officers (the lord advocate and the solicitor general). The lord advocate attends meetings of the cabinet only when requested by the first minister.

The Scottish Government operates on the basis of collective responsibility. This means that all decisions reached by ministers, individually or collectively, are binding on all members of the government. Collective responsibility does not mean that ministers must all agree on decisions; instead, membership of the government requires them to maintain a united front once decisions have been made.

In 2011, the Scottish Government had sixteen ministerial posts in all. There were six cabinet secretaries (including the first minister), ten ministers and two law officers – a total of eighteen, compared to a total of twenty for the previous administration.

Alex Salmond slimmed down the cabinet, claiming that his reorganised team was delivering a smaller, more effective government. In 2007 he had to find an entire ministerial team from only 47 MSPs, including deputy ministers and members of committees. Therefore, he reduced the size of the cabinet and ended the use of ministerial parliamentary aides (the equivalent to Westminster's parliamentary private secretaries).

The civil service

The civil service is a matter reserved by the UK Parliament and not a matter devolved to the Scottish Parliament. Therefore, the civil service in Scotland is part of the wider UK home civil service. While the permanent secretary of the Scottish civil service, Sir Peter Housden, is the most senior civil servant in Scotland and heads the strategic board of the Scottish Executive, he remains answerable to the most senior civil servant in the UK, the cabinet secretary. However, some people argue that those civil servants who work for the Scottish Government primarily serve the devolved administration rather than the UK Government.

To emphasise this, in 2007 First Minister Alex Salmond reorganised the structure of the Scottish civil service. Led by a permanent secretary, it

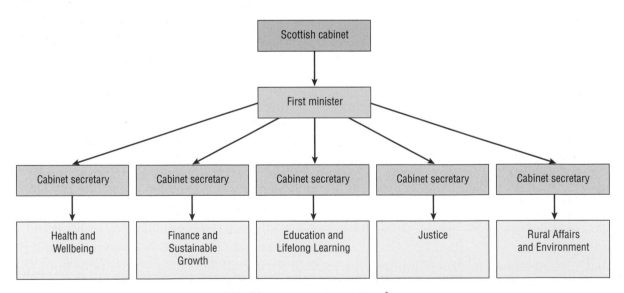

Figure 3.11 **The relationship between the cabinet and the civil service** ↑

has five directorates, each headed by a director-general, who together form a strategic board responsible for five strategic policy objectives of economy, environment, health, education, and justice and communities.

Arena for future conflict

Overall, it is the duty of civil servants to remain politically neutral, serve objectively and obey the government of the day. This is a duty to the office and not to the individual who holds that office; however, the effectiveness of government can be affected by the personal relationships between the office holder and the civil servant.

Furthermore, while the Civil Service Code (Scottish Executive Version) states that civil servants in Scotland are 'accountable to Scottish ministers who are, in turn, accountable to the Scottish Parliament', it advises that they are at the same time 'an integral and key part of the government of the United Kingdom'.

Therefore, the civil service in Scotland remains part of the UK home civil service. Nevertheless, some argue that civil servants working for the Scottish Government owe their loyalty to the devolved administration rather than to the UK Government.

Right now, civil servants in Scotland are working directly for an SNP administration and their colleagues in London are working directly for a Conservative–Liberal Democrat coalition administration. According to Scotland's former most senior civil servant, Sir John Elvidge, the election of the SNP has brought to an end the informal contact that used to be commonplace between the Scottish Executive and the UK Government when Labour was in control of both parliaments. This could lead to further conflict if London and Edinburgh were to begin operating as separate administrations, breaking the powerful civil service links that currently bind Scotland to the rest of the UK.

For government to work effectively, there must be open communication and trust between the two administrations. However, the core problem is that in reality the civil service is serving two governments of different political ideologies at the same time.

Therefore, a situation of conflict could develop when a civil servant serving a Conservative–Liberal Democrat coalition minister in Westminster has to talk to or brief a civil servant in Edinburgh who serves an SNP minister. If the matter is a confidential one, the exchange of details may be restrained and limited because they both know that the information will be shared with the opposing ministers. Sir John Elvidge highlighted this issue in 2007, commenting that informal contact had been reduced after a high-profile and public disagreement over the foot-and-mouth disease compensation issue. It became apparent that civil servants in Scotland and England were unwilling to reveal sensitive aspects of policy development to one another.

Implications of and demands for further devolution

While the SNP government in Scotland would like independence, they know that they could not push for this without holding a referendum. Originally they were committed to a referendum bill in 2010, and in the process leading up to this they launched a 'national conversation' on Scotland's future. The formal white paper or draft legislation laid out what the SNP saw as the three choices for the country's future.

1 Maintain the current devolved arrangement.
2 Extend devolution by increasing the powers of the Scottish Parliament.
3 Full independence.

It became clear that a referendum bill would not be supported by the 'Unionist parties', and so the SNP did not proceed with the bill. Labour and the Liberal Democrats were willing to grant further devolved powers to the Scottish Parliament and set up their own committee under Lord Calman.

This 'Unionist coalition' of the opposition parties changed the face of Scottish politics from one of right against left to one of nationalists against Unionists. The Unionists know that the only way to defeat the SNP's independence drive is through cooperation.

While none of the parties are happy with the current devolved arrangement, all the

---

Fact File

Scotland Bill (2010–11)

The UK Government proposes the largest transfer of fiscal power from London since the creation of the United Kingdom. The Scotland Bill will strengthen Scotland's future, by:

- Increasing the financial accountability of the Scottish Parliament
- Making devolution work better by ensuring that the Scottish Parliament and Scottish Ministers have the right powers
- Improving how the Scottish Parliament operates.

The Commission on Scottish Devolution (also known as the Calman Commission) was set up in 2007 to independently review the constitutional settlement for Scotland after a decade of devolution.

The Scottish Parliament will move from raising approximately 15% of its own budget to approximately 35%. The Bill will include power for the Scottish Parliament to put in place a Scottish rate of income tax. The tax paid by Scottish taxpayers will be derived from reducing the existing rates of income tax by 10 pence and adding a new Scottish rate amount on to each of the basic, higher and additional rates of tax.

The Scotland Bill will amend some areas of Schedule 5 to the Scotland Act 1998, which currently sets out what is reserved to the UK Parliament, including:

- Scottish Ministers to have powers in relation to the misuse of drugs
- Scottish Ministers to have powers relating to the administration of elections to the Scottish Parliament
- Power to regulate air weapons devolved to Scottish Parliament
- Scottish Ministers to have power to set regulations for the drink-drive limit
- Scottish Ministers to have the power to determine the national speed limit in Scotland.

The aim is for the Scotland Bill to complete its Westminster passage by November 2011 [and] to have the new tax powers in place by 2015, with income tax changes in 2016.

Extracted from www.scotlandoffice.gov.uk/scotlandoffice

opposition parties reject full independence but would like more powers for the Scottish Parliament. The Liberal Democrats want increased powers for the Scottish Parliament and more control over tax. Both Labour and the Conservatives also want increased powers, but Labour wants a limited form of fiscal federalism while the Conservatives are wary of transferring too much power.

In effect, the three main opposition parties are attempting to gain the upper hand and isolate the SNP by showing that they are willing to consider reforms, short of an independence referendum. In the end though, any changes to Scotland's powers or even full independence would involve changes to the Scotland Act and this can only be done by Westminster – Westminster must allow it for it to happen.

Scotland in the British constitution

The UK remains a unitary state. The constitutional relationship between the Scottish Parliament and the UK Parliament is defined clearly in section 28 of the Scotland Act (1998), which states that the Scottish Parliament's power to legislate 'does not affect the power of the Parliament of the United Kingdom to make laws for Scotland'. This means that Westminster could legitimately overrule or veto the enactments of the elected Scottish legislature.

The secretary of state for Scotland

In 1999, the Scottish Parliament took on the legislative powers for devolved matters, and ministerial functions for devolved matters were transferred to Scottish ministers who are accountable to the Scottish Parliament. Today, the Scottish Government is responsible for all devolved matters and most of the responsibilities previously held by the Scottish Office have become part of the remit of the Scottish Government. At the same time, the secretary of state for Scotland remains a member of the UK Government and is accountable to the UK Parliament.

Figure 3.12 Michael Moore MP, secretary of state for Scotland ↑

The secretary of state for Scotland holds this post jointly with another post in the UK cabinet. In addition to his other ministerial duties, he represents the interests of Scotland in the UK cabinet, particularly in those matters reserved to the UK Government. He is also responsible for the smooth running of Scotland's devolution settlement and acts as guardian of the Scotland Act.

Prime Minister David Cameron appointed Michael Moore, the Scottish Liberal Democrat MP for Berwickshire, Roxburgh and Selkirk, as Scottish secretary. This has been seen as a move to shore up the coalition government's legitimacy. The Liberal Democrats have eleven Scottish MPs at Westminster and the Conservatives only one.

Labour MPs have remained scornful of the appointment, accusing the Liberal Democrats of hypocrisy because they had pledged in their manifesto to abolish the Scottish Office.

Scotland's representation at Westminster

The results of the 2010 general election once again highlighted what critics of devolution regard as the unfairness of the arrangements. They claim that it didn't matter much to the people of Scotland who won the election because they have their own parliament and government, and pursue their own policies on many domestic and devolved issues. In addition, Scotland still got to send 59 MPs to Westminster, who can debate and vote on legislation that only applies to England. This is known as the West Lothian question.

The West Lothian question

It is argued that Scottish MPs could hold the balance of power at Westminster, and be able to wield significant influence over policies that could never affect Scotland or have an impact on their constituents. This has raised the question that if Scotland can elect a parliament that represents their views, and if Wales and Northern Ireland can elect assemblies to do the same, why can't England?

If there was a separate English Parliament after the 2010 UK election, it would contain 298 Conservative MPs, 191 Labour, 43 Liberal Democrats and 1 Green. That would add up to a Tory majority of 31, compared with being 19 short of a majority.

Implications for Scotland of government policies in reserved areas

The Scottish Parliament legislates for Scotland on devolved matters while the UK Parliament at Westminster continues to legislate for Scotland on reserved matters. However, in certain circumstances the Scottish Parliament may give its consent for Westminster to legislate for Scotland on devolved matters. This procedure is known as a Sewel motion or a legislative consent motion (see page 90).

Some government policies on reserved matters can have significant implications for Scotland through their potential impact on the policies of the Scottish Government, who will have to implement them in Scotland (for example, European Union regulations). They can also impact on the exercise of ministerial functions that are devolved and may need to take account of the separate Scottish legal system. The devolved and reserved powers are listed on page 80.

Financing the Scottish Government

How should the expenditure of the Scottish Government departments and their policies be financed? This is one of the most difficult questions facing politicians on both sides of the border. Differences of opinion over it can threaten good relations between Scotland and the rest of the UK. It is not a new question in so far as it has long been claimed that Scotland received more than its fair share of British public expenditure in the pre-devolution era. Treasury figures released in 2009 suggest that public expenditure per capita (the most common test of 'fairness') was higher in Scotland than in any other British 'region' except Northern Ireland. The amounts disclosed in Table 3.3 include expenditure by both British departments in Scotland and the Scottish Office.

Table 3.3 **Public expenditure by region, 2007–8**

Region	Expenditure per capita (£)
Northern Ireland	9577
Scotland	9032
London	9005
Wales	8493
UK	7675

Source: Public Expenditure Statistical Estimates (2009)

Such 'discrepancies' are partly based on different levels of deprivation across British regions. In respect of Scotland's apparently favoured and privileged position, part of the explanation lies in its relatively large territorial size and low population density outside the central belt, which means that expenditure per person for the same level of services such as education and health care is higher (Scotland's population is 10 per cent of England's).

Differences such as those shown in Table 3.3 continually stimulated political debate along regional and party-political lines while there was a Labour administration in Westminster and a Labour–Liberal Democrat coalition in Holyrood (1999–2007). For electoral and political reasons, Labour was sympathetic to Scottish claims that differences in expenditure were justifiable. Now, with an SNP administration in Holyrood and a Conservative–Liberal Democrat coalition in Westminster, there is an intensification of the controversy along national lines, with English regions renewing their complaint that they are unfairly treated and the Scots replying that the differentials are justifiable on the grounds of need and Scotland's contribution to the British Treasury from North Sea oil revenues. The ultimate catch-22 situation for any English politicians looking for a reduction in Scottish public expenditure is that reducing Treasury-sourced Scottish expenditure might strengthen the SNP's case for independence.

Relationships

Overall, the relationship between Scotland and the UK has remained good throughout the decade of devolution even while there has been a difference of party-political government.

The Scottish Government maintains very constructive working relations with the governments of the UK through what is known as a memorandum of understanding. This is a mechanism that enables ministers of the four administrations of the UK to meet and discuss policy issues together. It has led to the setting up of a Joint Ministerial Committee.

There are also more detailed concordats between the Scottish Government and individual UK Government departments. These concordats are non-legally-binding agreements whose purpose is to facilitate good relations between the administrations.

Nevertheless, fiscal restraint caused by the banking crisis and the emerging role of the coalition at Westminster may put these relationships to the test.

After the 2010 general election, the Queen's Speech voiced the intention of the coalition government to be more considerate and thoughtful towards Scotland. The prime minister had accused the Scottish and previous Labour governments of allowing a 'fractious relationship' to sour links between London and Edinburgh. He said that his government wanted a fresh start with the Scottish Nationalist government in an attempt to restore good relations between the Westminster and Holyrood parliaments. He said he wanted to pursue a 'respect agenda'.

Figure 3.13 David Cameron said he aimed to be more considerate towards Scotland ←

Scotland's budget

On coming to office, the UK chancellor George Osborne was adamant that the decade of growth of the Scottish Government budget, which had doubled since devolution, had to end. However, he did not impose any cuts on the Scottish Government's £30-billion-a-year block grant from the Treasury in his first year, claiming that his actions were 'a good example of the respect agenda in action'. He did identify future cuts of around £5 billion for Scotland, though.

Top of the coalition government's agenda was giving the Scottish Parliament significant new powers over income tax rates and additional legal powers on gun control, drink-drive limits and speed limits, as recommended by the Calman Commission.

The Barnett formula

Essentially the formula means that for every £1 the UK Government distributes, 85p goes to England, 10p to Scotland and 5p to Wales. With a population of five million people, Scotland has only around 8 per cent of the UK population but gets a fixed quota of 10 per cent of the cash for public services. That has led to a situation where spending in Scotland on public services is £1500 higher per person than in England.

English politicians and newspapers have criticised the formula as being unfair to England. On the BBC's *Question Time* and Radio Five Live, a *Daily Mail* columnist, Kelvin MacKenzie, declared that Scots were ripping off the English. He stated that 'basically the Scots exist solely on the handouts of the clever English generating wealth in London and the south-east'.

This viewpoint has been challenged in Scotland. The SNP highlights the 'Barnett squeeze'. It argues that rather than protecting the favourable spending position of Scotland, the formula is steadily eroding that advantage. They claim that if a 4 per cent increase in expenditure was required to make up for an increase in inflation, Scotland would only get an increase of 3 per cent of its total budget whereas England would get the full 4 per cent (based on a proportion of each country's population).

One crucial feature of the Scottish block grant is that it allows ministers to decide how the annual budget is spent. Expenditure is allocated *en bloc*, not per service (health, transport, etc.) – thereby giving ministers the opportunity to reallocate funds between services in line with their priorities.

The Calman Commission

The Conservative–Liberal Democrat coalition government pledged in 2010 to implement the findings of the Calman Commission. The Calman Commission would bring forth new fiscal accountability and responsibility for Scotland. Before, the Scottish Government had no link between spending and taxation, and thus between its decisions, consequences and economic growth.

Calman would give Scotland more control of its own revenue raising. Half of the income tax raised in Scotland, along with stamp duty, landfill tax and air passenger duty, would be collected by the Scottish Government and would form one third of its budget. This budget was formerly from a block grant, the size of which was settled by the Barnett formula.

The Calman Commission would lead to income tax in Scotland being cut by 10p, with the block grant cut by an equivalent amount. The Scottish Government would be able to set its own rate of income tax. If it did so at 10p overall then revenues would be brought back up to their previous level, leaving no change.

Also, under the provision of the Scotland Bill the Scottish Parliament would be able to raise £12 billion in taxes and borrowing. MSPs could set their own rates of income tax and stamp duty and borrow up to £2.7 billion. In return, the annual block grant from Westminster to Holyrood would be cut and MSPs would be directly responsible for raising about a third of the money they spend.

This increased borrowing power would help in capital projects like new roads, schools and the replacement Forth Road Bridge. Among a range of other powers devolved to MSPs would be the ability to introduce new Scotland-specific taxes such as a levy on plastic bags, and alterations to speed and drink-driving limits.

Changes are being phased in over a four-year period until 2016, as follows:

- In April 2012, the Office for Budget Responsibility will publish Scotland's income tax, stamp duty and landfill tax levels and the Treasury determined by how much the block grant was to be cut.
- From April 2013, Scottish ministers will be able to borrow 10 per cent of their capital budget annually to fund new buildings and roads.
- Devolution of stamp duty and landfill tax (a levy on waste that has been dumped) will begin in April 2015.
- In 2016, income tax changes will be introduced.

It should be noted that the SNP government is in negotiations to change aspects of the Calman Commission report (see page 106).

Conflict with Westminster

Release of the Lockerbie bomber (2009)

Figure 3.14 Abdelbaset Ali al-Megrahi was released by the Scottish Government on health grounds ↑

Prime Minister Cameron declared publicly that the decision to allow the Lockerbie bomber, Abdelbaset Ali al-Megrahi, to return to Libya on health grounds 'undermined' the UK's global standing. Firstly, at the Tory party conference he attacked the Scottish Government's release of al-Megrahi. He said the decision was 'wrong' and that 'nothing like that must ever happen again.'

Then, on a visit to the USA, he said the decision to free al-Megrahi had been 'profoundly misguided' and sought to distance himself from the Scottish Government's decision. During a radio interview, he said, 'I agree that the decision to release al-Megrahi was wrong. I said it was wrong at the time. It was the Scottish Government that took that decision. I just happen to think it was profoundly misguided. He was convicted of the biggest mass murder and in my view he should have died in jail. I said that very, very clearly at the time; that is my view today. But let's be clear about who released al-Megrahi … it was the decision of Scottish ministers.'

Closure of coastguard centres (2011)

The UK coalition government's announcement of plans to abolish Scotland's five coastguard centres and replace them with a single full-time control room sparked fury in Scotland. The SNP and Labour in Scotland have united in their opposition to the plans. The Conservatives and the Liberal Democrats have kept silent on the issue proposed by their coalition counterparts at Westminster. The issue is a reserved matter, and the Scottish Parliament is powerless to do anything about it.

First Minister Alex Salmond said that the plans would jeopardise maritime safety and Labour's Duncan McNeil called them 'not only daft but dangerous'.

Fossil fuel levy (2011)

Figure 3.15 The UK Government is now prepared to hand over the fossil fuel levy to Scotland ←

An early example of the new 'respect agenda' politics is the issue of the fossil fuel levy.

After years of conflict with Labour ministers, the Conservative–Liberal Democrat coalition government seems prepared to hand over a pot of money to Scotland known as the fossil fuel levy. While in power, Labour consistently refused to hand over the cash despite claims that it was Scotland's money. Almost £200 million is now held by Ofgem from the proceeds of the levy in Scotland.

The 2015 general election

Conflict arose in 2010 over the UK Government's decision to fix the next UK election for 7 May 2015 because it clashed with Holyrood elections scheduled for the same day. The Scottish Government were concerned that holding both elections on the same day in 2015 would cause confusion for voters and major logistical problems for parties and returning officers. This date is already fixed by law for the Scottish Parliamentary elections, which use a different voting system.

The Scottish Government moved the date of the next election for the Scottish Parliament to May 2016 instead of 2015. A spokesperson for the First Minister said that the lack of consultation on the part of the coalition government showed that they were 'pursuing an agenda of disrespect'.

The 2011 Scottish elections

Prime Minister David Cameron and First Minister Alex Salmond also clashed over the coalition government's decision to hold a UK-wide referendum on voting reform at the same time as the Scottish Parliamentary elections in 2011.

Alex Salmond said that holding the referendum on adopting the alternative vote (AV) system for Westminster elections did not meet with Mr Cameron's respect agenda because it 'undermined the integrity of the elections in Scotland'.

It meant that voters in Scotland had to handle three ballot papers: two for devolved elections (combining first past the post and a form of proportional representation) and one for the referendum.

Some contentious issues in the Scottish Parliament

Debate on the war in Iraq

The Scottish Parliament can and does debate reserved matters, even though it cannot legislate on them. While MPs at Westminster were waiting to be allowed to debate the crucial issue of whether there should be a fresh mandate from the United Nations before war was waged on Iraq, the Scottish Parliament was debating it – even though it had no direct responsibility for defence or foreign affairs.

Asylum seekers

Asylum is one of the few issues with local effects that is run entirely from London, rather than being a devolved matter.

Before its closure, campaigners against Dungavel (an asylum seekers' detention unit in

Figure 3.16 Dungavel asylum seekers' detention unit ↑

Scotland) called for the Scottish Executive to be given the power to close it or at least speak out against it. However, the Executive could only refer people to the UK Home Office because it has no powers in this area – immigration is a reserved matter.

There are around 1300 asylum seekers currently in Glasgow who are in danger of being forced to leave the city because the UK Border Agency (UKBA) is no longer prepared to pay Glasgow City Council to house them. The UK Home Office has cancelled a contract with the city council to house and support asylum seekers.

This has resulted in a stand-off between the UK Government and Glasgow City Council. It could be that the Home Office wants to reduce the overall number of asylum seekers in Glasgow because of the public outcry when they are removed.

A government spokesperson said, 'Over the years we've had the Dungavel protests, the Ay family, the Glasgow Girls, Precious Mhango and the demonstrations about the dawn raids.' Meanwhile, a Glasgow Council spokesperson said, 'We have made numerous attempts to renegotiate the contract but the UKBA has refused to accept our position.'

In addition, Westminster has refused Scotland the power to have a separate protocol on the forced removal of failed asylum seekers, despite objections to the continued use of dawn raids. Immigration is reserved to the UK Government, and the Scottish Executive has no power to act in the matter – even to the point of having to accept specialist teams being sent to Scotland to deal with asylum applications after concerns were raised in Scotland.

Trident

The UK Government has voted to renew Trident, the country's nuclear submarine system, while the whole Scottish Parliament voted against renewing it.

However, the issue of renewing Britain's nuclear deterrent is reserved by Westminster and as far as the UK Government is concerned the decision has been made. In retaliation, Mr Salmond has caused conflict by suggesting that because the matter is reserved and the Scottish Government cannot prevent the renewal programme, the UK Government should have to pay to transport the warheads through Scotland. He has done this because while defence is reserved, transport is a devolved matter.

RAF bases

Concern for the future of several RAF bases in Scotland has also been raised.

Figure 3.17 The demonstration against the closure of RAF bases in Scotland ↑

The UK Government has decided that RAF Kinloss in Moray will close and orders for the new Nimrod MRA4 surveillance aircraft have been cancelled. In July 2011 it was announced that RAF Leuchars in Fife would also close.

In a show of unity, the first minister and other main party leaders and various MSPs, MPs and council leaders held an event in protest at the threats. It was attended by around 7000 people.

Alcohol

In September 2010, the Scottish Government suffered a defeat in parliament over its plans for minimum alcohol pricing. The parliament's Health Committee backed a Conservative amendment to strike from the Alcohol Bill plans for a minimum price per unit of alcohol of 45p.

Labour's Jackie Baillie said, 'The facts are that the Scottish Government has not been able to get a parliamentary majority because they have lost the argument' and Tory health spokeswoman Mary Scanlon said, 'There is simply no political support for the SNP's blanket minimum pricing. These plans would penalise responsible drinkers, harm the Scotch whisky industry, cost jobs and are probably illegal.'

Figure 3.18 The Scottish Government suffered a defeat in parliament over its plans for alcohol pricing ↑

Release of the Lockerbie bomber

In September 2009, the Scottish Government suffered a defeat in parliament over its handling of the Lockerbie bomber's release. Opposition parties united in a vote to condemn the decision to free the terminally ill Abdelbaset Ali al-Megrahi on compassionate grounds. The move fell short of a vote of no confidence in the SNP government.

Leader debates

First Minister Alex Salmond was left out of the televised leaders' debates at the 2010 general election, despite the SNP's legal battle for his inclusion.

Independence referendum

In the previous parliament (2007–11), the SNP were forced to drop plans for an independence referendum amid overwhelming opposition.

Apologies

In November 2010, the Scottish Government suffered a defeat in parliament as finance secretary John Swinney apologised for his controversial handling of Holyrood's only tax-raising power. Opposition parties were angry that the SNP administration failed to share key information about the availability of the Scottish variable rate (SVR), which allows for a levy of up to 3p in the pound. During a debate at the Scottish Parliament opposition parties voted 77–46 against the government, accusing ministers of an 'abuse of power' and of misleading parliament. They called for a full investigation of the facts by the Finance Committee.

Swinney was forced to say sorry over the 'Tartan tax' row and the first minister later joined him, saying, 'I join in his apology, I join in that apology, I've apologised today, I apologise.'

Has devolution made a difference?

Until 2007, devolved policy in Holyrood mainly mirrored policy in Westminster, with the Sewel motion acting as an instrument for fast-tracking UK legislation into Scottish law and a means by which UK-wide uniformity on certain matters was ensured. It also enabled EU or international obligations to be ratified and helped to ease the legislative burden in Scotland, allowing for the prioritising of more urgent matters. There were two reasons for this. Firstly, Labour was the main party of government at Westminster and Holyrood until 2010 and potential problem issues were more often than not solved through party channels. For example, the Secretary of State for Scotland acted as a link between the Labour majorities in Westminster and Holyrood. Secondly, there has been significant civil service continuity, with civil servants working for the Scottish Executive being part of a common UK home civil service within Whitehall that is bound by a collegiality around pragmatic and informal relationships.

Policy divergence

However, devolution has made some significant difference in policy terms between Scotland and the rest of the UK.

The Scottish Parliament has led the way with some policy differences that have created a gulf between Holyrood and Westminster. The successful use of devolution by the Scottish Parliament to legislate caused UK-wide resonance and helped set the terms for future policy debate throughout the UK.

A good example of Westminster catching up with Holyrood is over the banning of smoking in public places and the creation of a children's commissioner. In Scotland, the ban on smoking in public places came into force on 26 March 2006; in England, it took almost another year and a half (July 2007). The contrast could not be starker.

While the UK cabinet struggled to agree a deal on banning smoking in workplaces, the Department of Health said ministers had tried to strike a balance between freedom of choice and protecting non-smokers. This was also tied to anxieties over criticisms of the 'nanny state' from the press, which did not happen in Scotland.

Also, a public health expert said England lacked a champion to push the case for a ban; in Scotland, the first minister gave it his full support.

Following the May 2007 elections, things have been less smooth. The election of an SNP administration introduced party-political conflict into intergovernmental relations. The difference in party majorities in Westminster and Holyrood puts a strain on the collegiality of the UK home civil service. There is a call for a separate Scottish civil service.

The SNP government has also been critical of the Sewel convention because they feel it does not allow the Scottish Parliament to have a say in a bill in Westminster that may have an impact on Scots Law. If the SNP push for changes to this procedure, it may lead to Scotland having to formulate all of its own policies from scratch and increase pressure on the parliamentary timetable.

Mr Salmond is also calling for the Scottish Parliament to be given extra powers over broadcasting in Scotland, which is a reserved matter for the UK Government. Most MSPs support broadcasting being devolved, and a commission is being set up to look into Scottish broadcasting. In June 2011 Mr Salmond criticised the Supreme Court which sits in London. The court has overturned some Scottish legal decisions, leading to critics arguing that the independence of the Scottish legal system is at risk.

Policy convergence

Despite some differences in policy between Holyrood and Westminster, there are also examples of policy convergence. For example, arrangements for incorporating Scottish issues into UK issues have transferred smoothly from the pre- to the post-devolution situation. However, in EU matters, despite the Scottish Government making a significant contribution to the debate on European regions at the European Convention on behalf of the UK, the Scottish Parliament remains unable to deal directly with the EU on issues such as health and the environment – even though these are devolved matters. As a result, the SNP are now beginning to seek a distinctive Scottish profile in Europe.

Policy successes and failures

The SNP minority government of 2007–11 was forced to reduce its planned legislative programme, claiming a lack of parliamentary majority as the cause of its inability to fulfil pre-election manifesto promises like introducing a local income tax and the abolition of student debt.

The SNP's abandoned manifesto pledges

Alex Salmond's government was unable to implement many of its 2007 manifesto pledges because it couldn't secure the support of other parties in the chamber. It tried and failed to introduce the following because of a lack of consensus:

- **Local income tax**: the SNP abandoned its flagship manifesto pledge to introduce a local income tax in Scotland.
- **Abolition of student debt**: despite the £2200 graduate endowment being scrapped, the core promise remained unfulfilled.
- **£2000 grants to first-time homebuyers**: the manifesto promise was dropped after the housing minister said the sum would not give effective help.

- **Smaller class sizes**: the Scottish Government was unable to deliver its manifesto pledge to cut class sizes.
- **Raising the age for off-sales alcohol to 21**: plans for a blanket ban on alcohol off-sales to anyone under 21 were watered down.
- **1000 extra police officers by 2011**: the number of police officers did increase, but fell just short of the 1000 promised.

Nevertheless, over the 2007–11 parliamentary term there were public policy successes including new rail and motorway infrastructure, support for renewable energy and freezing council tax.

SNP government 2011–16

The new government, energised by its mandate from the Scottish people, set out its priorities for 2011 and beyond. Calman would be renegotiated, a referendum on independence would be held perhaps as late as 2015, and flagship policies such as a minimum price for alcohol would go forward as a bill to tackle Scotland's alcohol problems.

After being elected first minister by the Scottish Parliament on 18 May 2011, Alex Salmond argued that Scotland needs more financial powers and called on Westminster to devolve borrowing powers, corporation tax, the Crown Estates and excise duty. The first minister also called for control over digital broadcasting and said Scotland must have increased influence in Europe. Mr Salmond wants his wishlist of new powers added to the Scotland Bill going through Westminster. A spokesperson for Scottish Secretary Michael Moore stated such requests would have to be backed up by 'solid evidence and detailed assessment'. Mr Salmond wants Holyrood to be given borrowing powers from 2012 rather than 2013, and to be able to borrow £5 billion rather than the proposed £2 billion.

Alex Salmond, speaking about constitutional change in May 2011:

'Whatever changes take place in our constitution, we will remain close to our neighbour. My dearest wish is to see the countries of Scotland and England stand together as equals. There is a difference between partnership and subordination – the first encourages mutual respect, the second breeds resentment.'

Composition of the new parliament

The number of women in the Scottish Parliament increased from 43 in 2007 to 45 in the 2011 elections (see Figure 3.19). The SNP's Tricia Marwick was elected the first female Presiding Officer, although Annabel Goldie stepped down as leader of the Conservative party.

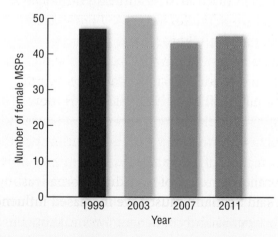

Figure 3.19 The number of female MSPs in the Scottish Parliament, 1999–2011 ↑

Two Asian MSPs were elected in the 2011 election.

Activities

1 Explain the difference between the Scottish Parliament and the Scottish Government.

2 Explain the difference between devolved and reserved matters.

3 Describe the founding principles of the Scottish Parliament.

4 How is committee membership determined?

5 Describe the work of committees.

6 Describe the different kinds of committees and provide examples.

7 What are the functions of committees?

8 What can committees do?

9 What are public and private bills?

10 Describe the legislative process.

11 Describe business in the debating chamber.

12 What is a legislative consent motion?

13 What is the Scottish Executive?

14 What is the Scottish Cabinet?

15 Describe the role of the civil service.

16 What is meant by the West Lothian question?

17 How is the Scottish Government financed?

18 What is meant by the memorandum of understanding?

Past exam questions

1 With devolution, there is no need for Scottish representation at Westminster. Discuss.

2 Assess the impact of devolution on decision making for Scotland.

Local government

The structure of local government in Scotland

Local government in Scotland is made up of 1222 elected councillors working on our behalf within 32 unitary authorities or councils. Some of these councils are based on county borders and cover a large geographical area while others are based on city boundaries – for example, Edinburgh and Glasgow. These local councils have a key role in communities and impact on the daily lives of all Scottish citizens. They provide vital public services, including schools for our children and care for the elderly; they also maintain our roads, collect our refuse and provide facilities for our leisure and recreation.

In addition, 45 related local authority organisations provide a further range of local public services, including police services, fire and rescue services and regional transport strategies. In fact, the range of services provided by our councils is extensive (see page 112) and the money to pay for them comes from a combination of council tax and grants from the Scottish Parliament, which in turn gets its money from the UK Government. Councils spend around £20 billion each year, employ around 250,000 staff and use assets worth about £32 billion. We elect paid councillors every four years to represent our interests and to manage these budgets.

Figure 3.20 shows Scotland's 32 unitary councils. In terms of population, the largest of these authorities is Glasgow City Council and the smallest is Orkney Islands Council.

The last 30 years have witnessed dramatic changes in the role, structure and influence of local councils. Under a UK Conservative government (1979–97), local authorities suffered a reduction in their income and range of services, which led to financial crisis and continual conflict with central government. The election of a UK Labour government in 1997 saw a new partnership with local authorities. The creation of a Scottish Parliament in 1999 under the control of a Labour–Liberal Democrat coalition (1999–2007) provided both opportunities and challenges for local councils to redefine their role and to restore their credibility with the Scottish people. The SNP minority government (2007–11) promised that they would work jointly with local councils towards agreed outcomes under a single national purpose. This concordat, agreed in November 2007, sets out the terms of the relationship between the Scottish Government and local government, based on mutual respect and partnership (see pages 116–117).

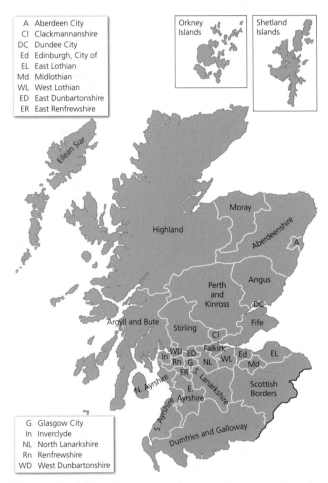

A	Aberdeen City
Cl	Clackmannanshire
DC	Dundee City
Ed	Edinburgh, City of
EL	East Lothian
Md	Midlothian
WL	West Lothian
ED	East Dunbartonshire
ER	East Renfrewshire

G	Glasgow City
In	Inverclyde
NL	North Lanarkshire
Rn	Renfrewshire
WD	West Dunbartonshire

Figure 3.20 Map of local government structures showing Scotland's 32 unitary councils ↑

Table 3.4 Scotland's local authorities: population and area

	Population	Area (km²)
Scotland	**5,194,000**	**77,925**
Aberdeen City	213,810	186
Aberdeenshire	243,510	6,313
Angus	110,250	2,182
Argyll & Bute	90,040	6,909
Clackmannanshire	50,540	159
Dumfries & Galloway	148,510	6,426
Dundee City	143,390	60
East Ayrshire	120,210	1,262
East Dunbartonshire	104,680	175
East Lothian	96,830	679
East Renfrewshire	89,240	174
Edinburgh, City of	477,660	264
Eilean Siar	26,180	3,071
Falkirk	152,480	297
Fife	363,460	1,325
Glasgow City	588,470	175
Highland	220,490	25,659
Inverclyde	80,210	160
Midlothian	80,810	354
Moray	87,660	2,238
North Ayrshire	135,510	885
North Lanarkshire	326,320	470
Orkney Islands	19,960	990
Perth & Kinross	145,910	5,286
Renfrewshire	169,910	261
Scottish Borders	112,680	4,732
Shetland Islands	22,210	1,466

	Population	Area (km²)
South Ayrshire	111,440	1,222
South Lanarkshire	310,930	1,772
Stirling	88,740	2,187
West Dunbartonshire	90,920	159
West Lothian	171,040	427

The councils have full responsibility for the provision of all the local government services with the exception of water and sewerage and the reporters to Children's Panels (the Scottish Children's Reporters Administration has responsibility for this).

There are three levels of government in Scotland: the Westminster government, the Scottish Parliament and local government. Local government is the democratically elected part of government in Scotland at the local level and has an interdependent relationship with the Scottish Government. The Scottish Government needs local government to provide services in accordance with their priorities; in return, local authorities expect the Scottish Government to provide the necessary financial resources to do so efficiently while maintaining a degree of political autonomy in order to adequately represent their local communities.

In 2010, the total expenditure by Scottish local government was around £20 billion. Almost 250,000 people were employed in local government in Scotland, including teachers, police officers, fire fighters and social workers.

This accounts for 60 per cent of all public sector jobs in Scotland. The next biggest public sector employer is the National Health Service (NHS), accounting for a third (33 per cent) of public sector jobs in Scotland.

Employment in local government

The number of staff employed by local authorities is gradually declining, and this pattern is set to continue in the short term. In 2010, the number of people employed in local government (including police and fire and rescue) was approximately 249,700. This was a reduction of around 3600 (1.4 per cent) compared with 2009. This includes reductions of 3.9 per cent in teaching staff, 0.7 per cent in social work, 0.6 per cent in other service areas and 1.8 per cent in fire and rescue services. Only police and related services, with 23,900 employed, saw no change over the same period. Further and bigger reductions are set to continue as councils respond to financial pressures.

Scottish local authority job losses set to exceed 10,000
February 2011

Thousands of local government jobs in Scotland are to be axed following council decisions on their budgets. Pat Watters, the president of the Convention of Scottish Local Authorities (COSLA), said that none of the 32 councils or any of the departments within them were likely to escape job cuts. It is expected that total local government job losses in Scotland will exceed 10,000 over the period 2011–15.

'Each authority is trying to keep job losses to a minimum but I would be very surprised if there are not job losses in every council,' he said. 'The reductions will be right across the board with councils trying to protect frontline services.'

Figure 3.21 Glasgow City Chambers ↑

Glasgow City Council, Scotland's biggest local authority, cut 2700 posts in 2011.

A spokesman for the city council said the job losses were being achieved through an early retirement package for those aged 50 or older and by voluntary agreement.

Edinburgh City Council will reduce its workforce by 1200 by 2014. This cut follows a 2.3 per cent staffing reduction in 2010, which included teachers.

Aberdeenshire Council plans to shed up to 900 posts, while North Lanarkshire Council is aiming to cut its workforce by 600 in an attempt to save £55 million. Neighbouring South Lanarkshire is due to lose 340 posts.

COSLA estimates that councils have lost a total of £450 million in funding because of a 2.5 per cent reduction in the amount local government receives from the Scottish Government.

Source: Chartered Institute of Public Finance and Accountancy

The role and function of local government

Local government in Scotland performs a range of functions. It is perhaps best known as a service provider, delivering services such as education, housing, social work, economic development, public protection, planning, and leisure and recreation facilities. However, local authorities also play a regulatory role, issuing licences for example to taxis and pubs, and providing regulatory services such as trading standards and environmental health. In addition, the local authority performs a community leadership role, promoting the interests of its local communities as well as fulfilling its statutory requirement to initiate and facilitate community planning.

Local authorities carry out their role within the powers prescribed under various Acts of the Scottish Parliament (see pages 113–117). Their functions are comprehensive, with some being mandatory. A mandatory service is one that the local authority is required by law to provide – for example, primary and secondary education.

More recently, local authorities have been required by law to ensure their service provision secures 'best value' and they must also facilitate community planning.

Others are discretionary. A discretionary service is one that the local authority is allowed to provide if it wishes – for example, providing an outing for elderly people.

Finally, others are permissive. A permissive service is one that the local authority is not required to provide by law but it is legally allowed to do so if it wishes – for example, swimming pools and theatres.

Provision of services

Local authorities are responsible for the planning, resourcing and direct provision of a wide range of services and are legally responsible for them. These services include education, housing, social work, economic development, public protection, planning, and leisure and recreation.

Local government has the additional responsibility to work in partnership with other public agencies and commissioning services from the voluntary and private sectors. This may include community planning partnerships and local economic forums.

For example, the Glasgow Community Planning Partnership operates across the local authority area to bring together a range of organisations that are committed to working together to ensure an inclusive Glasgow. It aims to provide more efficient and effective public services and to involve local communities in helping to decide what services are provided locally and how they wish to receive them. Glasgow City Council describes its community planning as 'the structure, processes and behaviours necessary to ensure that organisations work together and with communities to improve the quality of people's lives, through more effective, joined-up and appropriate delivery of services'.

The membership of the Glasgow Community Planning Partnership includes:

- Glasgow City Council
- Communities Scotland
- NHS Greater Glasgow
- Strathclyde Fire and Rescue
- Glasgow Housing Association
- Glasgow Chamber of Commerce
- Strathclyde Police.

Therefore, in order to fulfil its role of service provider, local government is now working more and more in partnership with the private and voluntary sectors, as well as with Scottish Government agencies such as Communities Scotland.

Case Study: Clean Glasgow

Clean Glasgow is a campaign to make Glasgow and its neighbourhoods cleaner and safer. It is built on a partnership with the Glasgow business community, Glasgow Chamber of Commerce, Communities Scotland and the *Evening Times* newspaper. Clean Glasgow has received £1 million in part funding from the Community Regeneration Fund, and businesses that support the campaign are helping to sustain the economic prosperity of Glasgow and make it an attractive place to live, work and visit. The manager of the Yell Group, who are involved, said: 'When we heard about Clean Glasgow we were very keen to become involved. As a company, we are considerate of the interests of the communities in which we operate and encourage our people to work with them to make a positive impact.'

Strategic planning

Local authorities publish a long-term strategic plan in which they lay out the long-term objectives for their local area and community. The purpose of these plans is to assess the priorities of local communities and look at how their needs can best be met. Therefore, strategic or community planning is a process whereby local authorities and other local agencies – including community, voluntary and private sector interests, for example businesses, charities and the NHS – come together to develop and implement a shared vision for promoting the well-being of their area.

Renfrewshire Council published its chief executive's service improvement plan for 2010–13, which outlined what the service intended to achieve over a three-year period based on the financial and employee resources available. The plan identified the principal factors that would influence service needs, their development and delivery. It also set out the main outcomes it hoped to achieve and laid out its strategic plan, prioritising its objectives to meet the needs of the local area and the people who live there.

Regulation

Local authorities have a regulatory function. Their role in regulation is to issue licences such as those to taxi drivers, shops and public houses. They also have the role of providing regulatory services such as trading standards and environmental health.

Community leadership

With the requirement on local councils to produce a strategic plan, it could be argued that local government is moving away from its traditional role as a service provider to one of community leader. Strategic planning combined with partnerships as a platform for the design and – more importantly – the delivery of services means that the council's role in providing services is diminishing as their role of co-ordinator of multi-agency provision increases. As their role and function changes, instead of being service providers local authorities are seeing themselves become strategic 'community leaders'.

The roles and functions have been determined by various Acts of Parliament, the most recent of which are outlined below.

Local Government in Scotland Act (2003)

The Local Government in Scotland Act (2003) is the key piece of legislation that the Scottish Parliament passed to modernise local government. It enables the delivery of better, more responsive public services that better meet the expectations of those who pay for and use them. It has the following provisions.

Figure 3.22 St Ninian's High School Kirkintilloch, one of five new schools in East Dunbartonshire ↑

Best value

The Act places all local authorities under a duty to secure best value. Best value is defined in loose terms to mean councils achieving continuous improvement in the performance of all their functions. The Act stresses that in securing continuous improvement in a particular service, councils are expected to maintain a balance between the quality and cost of the service delivered.

Many local authorities have used public–private partnerships (PPPs) to build new schools. East Dunbartonshire have built five new secondary schools under this scheme. Private consortia build and own the schools, which they rent out to the local authority. This provides state-of-the-art facilities for schools, with the downside that the local authority will be paying charges and interest for the next 30 years.

The SNP minority government is against PPPs and favoured alternative ways to find the capital to build new schools – the Scottish Future Trusts.

Best value and accountability

Duty to secure best value:

1 It is the duty of a local authority to make arrangements that secure best value.

2 Best value is continuous improvement in the performance of the authority's functions.

3 In securing best value, the local authority shall maintain an appropriate balance between (a) quality and (b) cost.

Community planning

The Act places duties on local authorities to initiate and facilitate community planning, and on core partners (health boards, the enterprise networks, police, fire and regional transport partnerships) to participate in the process. In addition, it places a duty on Scottish ministers to encourage community planning.

The power to advance well-being

The Act gives the local authority the power to do anything that it considers is likely to promote or improve the well-being of the area and/or people within that area, as long as it is not prohibited by existing legislation.

Local Government (Scotland) Act (2004)

The Local Government (Scotland) Act (2004) provided for the election of councillors by a form of proportional representation, the single transferable vote (STV). A related development was the creation of multi-member wards, consisting of three or four councillors; these electoral wards have increased in size and elected members now represent larger communities. However, the total number of councillors is unaffected, remaining at 1222 (see page 17).

The Act also established the Scottish Local Authorities Remuneration Committee (SLARC) to advise Scottish ministers on the payment of councillors.

Council committees

Decision making within Scottish local government is carried out by individual councils that are made up of councillors, who are elected every four years. These elected members are led by the leader of the council, typically the leader of the largest single political grouping in the council. Each council also elects a civic leader, the provost or convener, who chairs council meetings. In the cities of Glasgow, Edinburgh, Aberdeen and Dundee, the provost is known as the lord provost. The full council meeting is the sovereign body of the council, where all councillors meet to debate and take the key decisions of the authority. These include electing the convener and deputy convener, appointing councillors to all committees and panels, deciding on strategic objectives and corporate policies, and setting the annual budget and council tax levels.

While the full council is the supreme decision-making body in a local authority, the Local Government (Scotland) Act 1973 permits local

Benefits of the committee system

- It is inclusive: all political parties and independents of the council are represented on committees. This prevents council decisions being taken by people from one party alone (although the balance of representation on committees tends to reflect the balance of representation in the council as a whole).

- It prevents individual elected members becoming all-powerful and detached from other members.

- It operates through collective decision making, so the convener of a committee has to persuade its members to come to a joint decision.

- Because committees usually meet in public, the process allows transparency in the decision-making process.

Source: Government Improvement Service

Drawbacks of the committee system

- Decision making by committee can be a slow process. Because committees have to bring together a large number of elected members, their meeting cycles tend to be between four weeks and two months.

- Because they are inclusive and transparent, committees can result in lowest-common-denominator decision making.

- They fulfil both the decision making and the scrutiny function within the council, but arguably it is impossible to do both well.

Source: Government Improvement Service

authorities to devolve most decision making to a committee or sub-committee. Traditionally, local authority decision making has taken place within a structure of committees and sub-committees.

Glasgow City Council created controversy with its decision to set up 'arm's-length external organisations' (ALEOs) to deliver public services such as housing repairs and the maintenance of car parks. Councillors who sit on these organisations receive extra payments, and in 2010 it was disclosed that Glasgow City Council paid £400,000 to councillors in such a way. Glasgow is the only council that provides extra payment. The biggest ALEO earner is Anne McTaggart, who sits on three of these bodies and collects more than £19,000. These organisations were set up by the disgraced former Glasgow Labour leader, Stephen Purcell. Critics argue that these agencies do not represent best value and were used by Purcell to reward loyal councillors. In June 2011 the Scottish government announced that these payments would end.

Councillors receive a salary of about £16,000, and councillors who carry out senior roles receive enhanced payments. Councillors would rightly argue that they deserve to receive a salary given the amount of time they devote to their duties.

Local government officials

All local authorities in Scotland appoint a chief executive, who is head of the management team of directors of departments. In Renfrewshire Council, the chief executive has his or her own department that covers the key corporate responsibilities of the council.

The traditional view of the relationship between councillors and officials is that councillors make policy that officials implement, in the same way that civil servants carry out the wishes of the prime minister and the cabinet. In other words, power rests with the elected councillors.

An alternative view is that senior officials are involved in policy making. Directors of education, social work, finance, etc. have technical and professional expertise that councillors lack. Given the continuity of senior officials in office and the part-time nature of the councillors' role, it is not surprising that officials can influence policy making. It is important that senior officials have a good working relationship with senior councillors.

The concordat and single outcome agreements

The Scottish Government's concordat agreement with local government in 2007 changed the relationship between the two parties and led to a sizeable shift in decision making from national to local government. Today this relationship is based on mutual respect and partnership, promoting progress towards the alignment of funding and activities within local authorities and other areas of the public sector with the Scottish Government's priorities and national outcomes. Furthermore, the development of single outcome agreements (SOAs), which give local authorities greater freedom to set their own priorities, is an important part of these changes.

SOAs set out the 'outcomes which each local authority is seeking to achieve ... reflecting local needs, circumstances and priorities, but are also related to the relevant national outcomes' (Scottish Government).

SOAs consist of a mix of national and local outcomes. Under the terms of the partnership, the Scottish Government will set the direction of policy and the over-arching outcomes that the public sector in Scotland will be expected to achieve. It also provides the cash sums specified

COSLA

COSLA is the collective and representative voice of Scottish local government. Because there is only one tier of local government, with 32 unitary authorities, COSLA

Figure 3.23 COSLA represents Scottish local government ↑

represents the legitimate tier of democratically elected government that is closest to the people of Scotland, and the administrative body below the Scottish Parliament and Scottish Executive. All of Scotland's 32 local authorities are members of COSLA, with each electing councillors to represent them. COSLA meets on a regular basis throughout the year; its main headquarters in Edinburgh are staffed by professionals who are experienced in local government.

COSLA has two key roles: a representative role and an employers' role.

Representative role

COSLA represents local government interests to the Scottish Parliament and the Scottish Government. It does this by facilitating a platform for discussion and communication between its 32 member councils and the Executive and Parliament.

Employers' role

COSLA acts as an employers' organisation for Scottish local authorities, negotiating on salaries and conditions of service for local government employees between trade unions and the employees of local authorities. It also deals with industrial relations and employee development issues.

in the concordat. In return, local government will contribute directly to the delivery of the key commitments listed. In the past this has meant working within the constraints of a freeze on council tax as well as pressures to meet outcomes with the money provided. However, underpinning the concordat is the concept of partnership working to achieve improved outcomes.

In the past, the Scottish Government limited local government spending decisions by allocating funding to specific initiatives (ring-fencing). Now local authorities can decide on their own spending priorities and allocate funding as they see fit, giving them greater fiscal autonomy. Unfortunately for education, money once allocated to specific learning initiatives – for example, spending on textbooks – has been used by local authorities for other purposes, such as social work. This partly explains why 3000 permanent teaching posts have disappeared since 2007. In contrast, direct funding to the police authorities has led to a significant increase in the number of police officers. It is not surprising that teaching unions have argued that local authorities are too small to deliver education and that control over education should be taken away from councillors.

Nevertheless, at times the nature of the relationship and partnership working of the concordat have come under severe strain (see 'Playing with fire can be risky', page 118). Mike Russell, the SNP education secretary, has been accused of interfering in Argyll Council's 2011 school primary closure proposals.

The concordat agreement

The 2007 concordat reduced ring-fencing and devolved control of some budgets to local authorities and community planning partnerships. The intention was to ensure the alignment of funding and activities within local authorities and other areas of the public sector with the Scottish Government's priorities and national outcomes. To achieve this aim, the following four key tenets are included in the concordat.

- Collaborative working and joint accountability: the relationship between central and local government is based on mutual respect and partnership, and enables local authorities to respond more effectively to local needs.

- Finance and funding: financial decisions are taken locally and ring-fencing is reduced.

- Reduced bureaucracy: less micro-management by central government.

- SOAs: align local policy with overall government targets, taking account of local priorities.

Playing with fire can be risky

The concordat between Scotland's 32 local authorities and the SNP government was billed as giving councils greater flexibility over their budgets and furthering the devolution of decision making. However, the mutual respect and partnership that were the basis of the agreement appear to have gone up in smoke over the future of Scotland's eight fire services.

In February 2011 the justice secretary, Kenny MacAskill, announced a consultation process on whether to retain eight fire services and police forces, reduce the number on a regional basis or move to a single service for each. However, his comments implied that the Scottish Government had already decided that they wanted a single fire service before discussions were underway.

Figure 3.24 Kenny MacAskill MSP ↑

This brought an accusation from Councillor Pat Watters, president of COSLA, that the government had ignored the fact that fire and rescue is a local government function and should not be dictated by central government. The concordat was intended to facilitate a genuine partnership between central and local government, but Councillor Watters's comments come because councillors were ignored and the reports of the fire service boards disregarded.

Source: Extract from *The Herald* (1 February 2011)

Relations between local and national government

In June 1997, the UK Government signed the Council of Europe's Charter of Local Self-Government, thereby affirming its commitment to maintaining a strong system of local government. Central government must ensure the political, administrative and financial independence of local authorities and allow them the ability to manage local affairs under their own responsibility. Therefore, in theory local authorities should be independent bodies who are left alone to manage their daily business affairs without interference from the Scottish Parliament or Scottish Government.

In reality, however, the Scottish Parliament sets the agenda for most of the functions carried out by local authorities through Acts of Parliament; the Scottish Government sets the parameters of government policy for local government to put into practice, and also sets targets for local government to achieve.

For this relationship to work effectively, there must be cooperation between all levels of government. Scottish government ministers meet regularly with individual local authorities or with COSLA on specific and general matters of current interest or concern. Advice and help is also provided to local authorities by the Scottish Government departments.

This provides the potential for conflict between two democratic legitimacies: on the one hand, the democratic legitimacy of Scotland's 32 local authorities; on the other, the democratic legitimacy of both the Scottish Parliament and the Scottish Government.

The government needs local councils to implement government policy. Likewise, local authorities need the Scottish Government to give advice and assistance on their functions because of the legal constraints within which they must operate. More importantly, local government is reliant on the Scottish Government for income through the revenue support grant.

Similarly, good relations between local government and the Scottish Parliament are vital because it is Holyrood that legislates for Scotland. For this reason, relationships between local authorities and MSPs – especially constituency MSPs – have been important in the past and will continue to be in the future. This also involves COSLA as the main vehicle by which all councils seek to influence both MSPs and the Scottish Government.

In the past, especially under an SNP minority government, good working relationships have been critical. Effective leadership and governance at a local level have been dependent on good working relationships between MSPs, councillors and council officials, a shared commitment to national and local priorities and constructive debate leading to clear decision making.

Under the minority SNP government of 2007–11, this relationship came under severe strain as a result of competing demands on finances and substantial changes affecting how councils operated. Twenty-seven out of 32 local authorities were in political coalition and all had multi-member wards. Tensions rose over levels of emphasis on partnership working and new ways of delivering services.

Financing local government

Local government receives most of its income (around 80 per cent) directly from the Scottish Government in the form of grants. The remaining 20 per cent is raised locally by the council itself from council tax payments and various fees and charges for the services they provide (see Figure 3.25). It is for each local authority to set its council tax level depending on its own spending decisions and in consultation with local electors. With the introduction of the concordat, the Scottish Government has

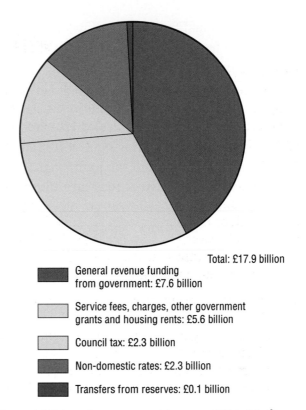

Total: £17.9 billion

■ General revenue funding from government: £7.6 billion

□ Service fees, charges, other government grants and housing rents: £5.6 billion

□ Council tax: £2.3 billion

■ Non-domestic rates: £2.3 billion

■ Transfers from reserves: £0.1 billion

Figure 3.25 Local government income, 2009–10 ↑
Source: Audit Scotland 2011

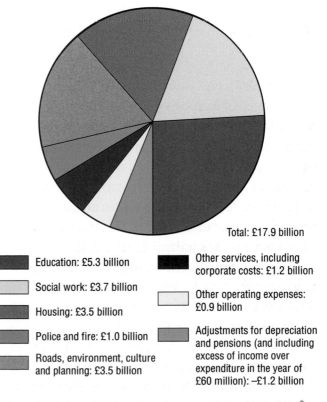

Total: £17.9 billion

■ Education: £5.3 billion

□ Social work: £3.7 billion

■ Housing: £3.5 billion

■ Police and fire: £1.0 billion

■ Roads, environment, culture and planning: £3.5 billion

■ Other services, including corporate costs: £1.2 billion

□ Other operating expenses: £0.9 billion

■ Adjustments for depreciation and pensions (and including excess of income over expenditure in the year of £60 million): –£1.2 billion

Figure 3.26 Local government expenditure, 2009–10 ↑
Source: Audit Scotland 2011

provided additional funding to allow local authorities to freeze their council tax levels.

The concordat recognises that it is the responsibility of each local authority to allocate the total financial resources available to it (excluding ring-fenced resources) on the basis of local needs and priorities, having first fulfilled its statutory obligations and the jointly agreed set of national and local priorities including the Scottish Government's key strategic objectives. Therefore, local authorities decide their own expenditure priorities from the income available to them and set their own council tax levels.

Support for the three-year revenue grant settlements is determined through negotiation between Scottish ministers and COSLA as part of the spending review process, which takes place every two or three years depending on the corresponding spending review timetable of the UK Government. The total revenue support is made up of three components: specific ring-fenced grants, non-domestic rate income (NDRI) and general revenue grant (GRG).

In order to ensure a fair and equitable distribution between councils, some local authorities receive more money from the Scottish Government than others. This is because not all local authorities are the same size and therefore do not have the same revenue-raising potential. For example, the largest local authority is Glasgow City Council, which has a population of almost 600,000; the smallest local authority is Orkney, with a population of fewer than 20,000.

Also, Glasgow is home to seventeen of the twenty poorest areas in Scotland, with the top ten most deprived council wards in Scotland all being in the city. Just over half of Glasgow's population lives in these most deprived areas. The four authorities with the next biggest proportions of deprivation are Inverclyde (39.1 per cent), Dundee (30.7 per cent), West Dunbartonshire (26.3 per cent) and North Ayrshire (25 per cent).

In addition, Scotland's 32 local authorities are diverse with differing expenditure needs, ranging from the four large and heavily populated city authorities to the small, sparsely populated rural and island authorities (see Figure 3.20 on page 108 for a map of Scotland's local authorities).

For example, the City of Edinburgh receives 75 per cent of its income in grants from the Scottish Executive and raises the additional 25 per cent itself from council tax and fees and charges, while Comhairle nan Eilean Siar on the Western Isles receives 92 per cent from the Scottish Executive and only raises 8 per cent by itself from council tax and fees and charges.

The levels of aggregate external finance (AEF) are set by the Scottish Executive during a spending review that takes place every two years and leads to a settlement to cover a three-year period. This AEF is funding that is determined by central government and is outwith council control. Allocated to each local authority by the Scottish Government to help finance the cost of services, AEF comprises the revenue support grant, business rate income and ring-fenced grants. The three-year settlement allows local authorities to plan their expenditure priorities with some stability and certainty. The equalisation mechanism is 'needs-based' and in proportion to the diverse characteristics of local council areas.

Fees and charges

This includes payments to the local authority for the provision of services such as nursing and residential care homes, school meals, sports facilities, parking and trade waste collection.

Case Study: Aberdeenshire Council's income

In 2011, Aberdeenshire Council complained that it lagged far behind the rest of Scotland in terms of government grant per head of population. Its grant for 2011–12 was 12.6 per cent below the Scottish average. Like all other Scottish councils, it agreed to a freeze in council tax for 2011–12 and the delivery of key policy outcomes in return for a reduction in grant of 2 per cent. Failure to agree to these conditions would have led to a much larger cut of around 6.4 per cent.

Table 3.5 **Aberdeenshire Council's projected sources of income (£ million)**

	2011–12	**2012–13**	**2013–14**	**2014–15**
Revenue support grant	341.0	328.9	330.6	332.2
Business rates	68.3	68.3	68.3	68.3
Ring-fenced grants	17.2	17.2	17.2	17.2
Fees and charges	38.0	38.0	38.0	38.0
Council tax	116.5	117.6	118.7	119.9
Total	**581.0**	**570.0**	**572.8**	**575.6**

- ring-fenced grants: 3 per cent
- fees and charges: 6 per cent
- business rates: 12 per cent
- council tax: 20 per cent
- revenue support grant: 59 per cent

Source: Aberdeenshire Council

Expenditure

Local government expenditure is split between revenue and capital expenditure.

Revenue expenditure is largely made up of employee and operating costs. Capital expenditure is mainly incurred by local authorities for buying or investing in large assets that will be of benefit to the community over many years – for example, roads, schools and other buildings. It is mainly financed from grants, loans and the proceeds from the sale of surplus assets.

Costs increased in 2009–10 and again in 2010–11 because of the severity of the winter weather and its toll on roads, as well as meeting increased social care demands. Major areas of capital spending were housing and schools estates (including building programmes and refurbishment work). Other areas included community and leisure facilities, social work and care facilities, and infrastructure.

Paying for local services – the debate

The way that local councils pay for the local services they provide has always been the topic of much debate. As stated earlier, local government receives around 80 per cent of its income directly from the Scottish Executive in the form of grants. The remaining 20 per cent is raised locally by the council from council tax payments and various fees and charges. It is the method of collecting this extra 20 per cent that is the cause of disagreement. Although council tax levels have been frozen since 2007, each local authority has the power to set its own level. This has resulted in significant variations in the average council tax levels between Scotland's 32 local authorities. For example, in 2010–11 the highest level of band D council tax was charged in Aberdeen (£1230) and the lowest was Eilean Siar in the Western Isles (£1024).

According to the Scottish Government, in 2009–10 for Scotland as a whole the total amount of council tax billed was £1.963 billion. Of this total, £1.855 billion was collected. This is a collection rate of 94.5 per cent. The collection rates across authorities ranged from 91.4 per cent to 97.7 per cent. Between 1993–94 and 2009–10, the overall total amount of council tax billed in Scotland was £24.317 billion, of which £23.361 billion (or 96.1 per cent) was collected.

Most reform of local government is dependent on the ability of local authorities to raise their own finance to pay for services, mainly from council tax. A centrally imposed freeze breaches local authority autonomy. Nevertheless, in 2011 all four major parties supported this. The Liberal Democrats claimed to dislike the idea, favouring a local income tax. The Conservatives had backed previous freezes and wanted to extend it followed by local plebiscites if a council planned an increase above the rate of inflation. They also offered a £200 council tax discount for households where all the adults are pensioners. The SNP were keen to continue to prepare the ground for a local income tax once enhanced powers over income tax and council tax benefit were devolved.

However, councils are fiercely protective of their powers and any subsequent council tax freezes will not be accepted without a fight. It has been suggested that there are two ways to overcome local authority opposition. One is to legislate to enforce a council tax freeze. But such a move would risk open conflict between councils and the Scottish Government. It could be seen as a move to take power away from councils and place it in the hands of central government.

A second option is the kind of carrot and stick approach that was used to freeze the council tax between 2007 and 2011. Essentially this meant making the kind of offer to councils that would have made it hard for them to increase the council tax while maintaining their right in principle to do so. Councils were given extra money each year to cover the costs of freezing the council tax. If a council had wanted to put the tax up, it would have lost this extra cash so the increase would have to be even higher. In 2010–11, the offer to councils was more stark: a cut in government cash if the council tax was frozen; a far bigger cut if it was not.

COSLA said that the estimated £700 million councils have been given since 2007 to freeze council tax was not a realistic estimate of the true losses that the policy imposed on the authorities, which could be up to double that figure. It highlights the opposition of council leaders to freezes and it believes they will not sign up to future council tax freezes. COSLA predicts a £1.7 billion black hole in public finances by 2013–14 that could rise to £2.8 billion by 2017. This figure is the estimated gap between income for local government, which is falling, and the steep rise in demand created by demographic changes, including the fact people are living longer and making more demands on health and social care budgets.

An April 2011 *Sunday Herald* investigation showed that the council tax freezes have disproportionately benefited the wealthy. Instead of helping the poorest in society, as was intended, the freeze has given the biggest reductions to the well off. It found that between 2007 and 2011 the households at the top of the rating scale (in band H) saved an average of £441 each while the cheapest homes (in band A) saved only £147.

With councils facing 12 per cent budget cuts by 2014, financial experts and politicians are now calling for a review of the freeze or an end to it because they fear services will be cut

if authorities can't raise more in tax. In West Dunbartonshire, the SNP-led council claims it faces cuts of at least £12 million a year between 2011 and 2014.

Council leaders say that political parties need to review how local government is to be financed, claiming that it is becoming more and more difficult to justify spending a declining budget on freezing council tax.

Reform of local government: What the political parties say

Figure 3.27 Scotland's political parties disagree on how best to reform local government ↑

Scottish Conservatives

- The Conservatives want to keep the council tax but the concordat will be abolished and replaced with a requirement upon councils to set out their own plans and report on progress within a new funding formula for local government. In order to make savings while protecting frontline services, the Accounts Commission will report on the extent to which each council shares services with other public sector bodies.

- Local authorities will be required to allocate a budget to community councils, proportionate to the size of the area they cover, so that more community councils may undertake their own projects.

- In Scotland's four largest cities (Glasgow, Edinburgh, Aberdeen and Dundee), renewed and accountable local leadership will be encouraged by giving people the chance to have a powerful, elected provost through a system of referenda.

Scottish Liberal Democrats

- The Liberal Democrats prefer a local income tax as an alternative to the council tax, although they do support a council tax freeze.

They will introduce a 'fairer local funding action plan', which will:

- Review the funding formula for local government to make it simpler, more transparent and fairer to all authorities.

- Introduce progressively a new rule to ensure that no authority receives less than 90 per cent of the average revenue support grant per head.

- Promote greater local democratic oversight of public spending and joint working.

- Support and assist those local authorities who want to propose a regional option to public services, but will not impose a centrally driven reorganisation of local government.

SNP

- The SNP want to introduce a local income tax to replace the council tax.

- Reform the relationship between central and local government.

- Introduce a Community Empowerment and Renewal Bill, which they claim will make it easier for communities to take over underused or unused public sector assets, and include measures to enable communities to deal more effectively with derelict or unused property in their area.

Scottish Labour Party

- Labour will introduce reforms required to deliver the intended benefits of shared services. The Scottish Futures Trust will be abolished, to be replaced with an Infrastructure Investment Unit.

- Local democracy will be enhanced with participation in community planning partnerships, ensuring that a diversity of voices is heard in community planning processes.

- A new process of consultation will be introduced through which an accord between central and local government will be delivered, based on the principles of mutual respect, transparency and accountability, to all stakeholders where national goals lend themselves to local priorities.

Scottish Green Party

- The Scottish Green Party will scrap the council tax and business rates and replace them with a land value tax. The party argues that taxing the value of the land rather than the value of the property on it encourages suitable developments.

- More powers would be devolved down from Holyrood to local councils to give local people greater control about how money is raised and spent.

- Reforms will enhance the support councils get to raise more of their own cash, including community-owned projects, and allow councils to merge.

(Adapted from 2011 Scottish Parliament elections party manifestos)

Reform of local government

Future demands and resource pressures on local authorities

Local government now faces a long period of working with reduced budgets. The combined effect of cuts in budgets and increasing demand for services means that councils face some very difficult decisions in order to link resources to priorities while demonstrating value for money. A key challenge will be to balance the need to find savings with that of maintaining the range and quality of the services they provide.

This reduced financial position requires a clear focus on budgets alongside councils' ongoing statutory requirement to achieve best value – that is, continuous improvement. The best value principles are as important now as they have ever been, although the emphasis will shift to improving service areas that individual councils identify as priorities and providing value for money and good-quality services with fewer resources.

There is great pressure on councils to maintain the current quality of their services to their users' satisfaction as they look to find savings in their budgets. Table 3.6 shows the demand and resource pressures faced by councils.

Sharing services

Future sharing of council services could contribute to more efficient and effective public services. Tayside Contracts is an example of collaboration between councils. It is a commercially based local authority contracting organisation providing catering, cleaning, roads maintenance, vehicle maintenance and winter

Table 3.6 Demand and resource pressures on local authorities

Demand pressures	Resource pressures
Increasing numbers of older people – pressure on social care services	Reducing revenue budget
Waste management targets – pressure on environmental services	Reducing capital budget
Economic pressures: ● increasing benefit claimants ● pressures on welfare and advice services ● increasing demand on social housing ● increasing demand on school places ● increasing demand on economic regeneration services ● increasing demand on business advice services	Economic pressures: ● reducing income from non-domestic rates ● reducing income from capital receipts ● reducing income from capital deposits and short-term investments ● reducing income from planning and building control fees ● increasing borrowing costs
Local pressures: ● flooding ● increasing winter maintenance	Carbon management: ● investment needed by councils to meet emissions targets ● removal of ability to recycle allowances in Carbon Reduction Commitment Energy Efficiency Scheme
Equal pay commitments	
Pension commitments	

Source: Audit Scotland

maintenance throughout the Tayside area. It is a collaboration between the councils of Angus, Dundee City, and Perth and Kinross; it operates under a joint committee comprising elected members from each constituent council.

Other initiatives at a national level include the joint development of the myjobscotland recruitment portal (www.myjobscotland.gov.uk) and the public information notices portal, with COSLA estimating overall savings of between £3 million and £4 million per year. Also, the group of eight councils that form the Clyde Valley Community Planning Partnership are looking to share services in seven areas: waste management, health and social care, social transport and fleet management, property sharing and management, support services, charging and economic strategy.

Edinburgh City Council – shared services

Edinburgh City Council has embarked on a shared service and collaborative working arrangement with other councils in south-east Scotland. The group has agreed to focus its activities on those areas with the greatest potential to deliver savings and improvement. These are: payroll/HR, mobile/flexible working, procurement and (potentially) roads maintenance.

Activities

1 Describe the structure of local government in Scotland.

2 Describe the role and function of local government in Scotland.

3 Describe the benefits and drawbacks of the committee system in Scottish local authorities.

4 What is the role of COSLA?

5 Describe the relationship between local and national government in Scotland.

6 Describe in detail from where local authorities receive their income.

7 What is meant by revenue and capital expenditure?

8 Describe the problems faced by local authorities in paying for local services.

9 How do each of the major parties intend to reform local government in Scotland?

10 Describe the future demands and resource pressures on local authorities.

11 Describe what is meant by partnership working.

12 Describe what is meant by sharing of services.

Essay question

Critically examine the role of local government in a devolved Scotland.